Practical Excel® 2010

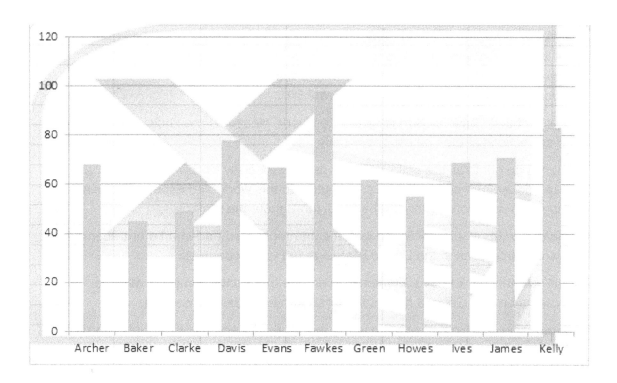

Copyright © 2016 by Justin Holt

First Printing: 2016

ISBN 978-1-326-56963-1

Ottersholme

277 Long Lane, Huddersfield, West Yorkshire HD5 9SH

www.practicalexcel2010.com

Acknowledgements & Notifications

I would like to thank everyone involved in the creation and development of this work.

I am especially grateful to those many friends and colleagues who have contributed by asking questions for me to help with, to those who have freely been providing me with information, drawings and photographs. Where possible, I have acknowledged original artists and photographers. Some items have been provided under the GNU free documentation licence and creative commons licences (http://creativecommons.org/licenses/by-sa/2.5/).

In the event that I have incorrectly attributed work, please let me know, allowing me to make corrections at the earliest opportunity.

My thanks go out to all the entire editorial team, especially to Oswald Spencer and Barney Booker for their invaluable contribution to this work, and especially to Kath, for keeping the team working together so well throughout the project.

About the Author

Justin Holt has been using MS Windows® and Excel® since 1990, and is constantly amazed that this is before many of his colleagues had even started school.

He had finished his college studies before PCs were available for consumers and was used to writing COBOL and ALGOL programmes input using punch cards. He has seen many innovations in IT, but considers the very wide uptake of the computer in education and industry as being the most important.

After an early career in sales and marketing management, the recession at the end of the 80's forced a rethink and a change of direction. The outcome is that Justin is now an IM&T project management professional working in healthcare.

Outside of work and computing he has maintained a nerdy interest in popular science, aviation history and sports. He is a veteran martial artist, and has the aches and pains to prove it. He also writes.

Justin is a Romford boy by birth and upbringing, but now lives in West Yorkshire, England. This may account for some unexpected phrases and spellings. Despite his odd accent, he has tried to use the Queen's English throughout. He unreservedly apologies for any confusion that this may cause those not from the UK, but thinks that if you are smart enough to buy and work through this book, then 'appen you are more than smart enough to deal with a few differently spelt words and strange phrases. Sorted!

He really hopes that you find this volume useful and that it makes your work a bit easier than it was before you bought the book.

Contents

Introduction

Practical Excel 2010 has been written with you in mind from the very beginning. I wrote thinking of everyone who has ever asked me how to solve an Excel problem or to show them how to do something. I've included many of these real world issues in the text.

Users new to Excel will be able to quickly create really useful spreadsheets by following the text and viewing the clear screenshots which will guide you through all the tasks. More experienced users may prefer to dip in and out to find specific topics.

This book is laid out so that you can follow along in easy steps, with a heavy emphasis on the pictures showing you what to click. Your version of Excel may differ from the version used here, or be customised differently, and could mean your screens don't match exactly. Don't stress, they shouldn't differ drastically.

You may notice that some dialogue boxes may differ slightly from the ones you have. This may well be the difference between Windows 2007 and Windows 10. They shouldn't cause you any trouble.

I've made a few thwapping great big assumptions about you. These are that you know how to open up your computer and can find your way around Windows and also have an installed copy of Excel 2010. If these aren't all true, then you may need to reconsider your purchase. I'd rather keep you as a happy future reader when all these preconditions exist than have you be unable to use this book for now.

You may already know that Microsoft often has 2 or 3 ways to achieve the same result. I aim to introduce these to you, but you get to decide the best way that you want to work.

There is a website that compliments this text (www.practicalexcel2010.com). You will find plenty to interest you, including articles, videos, a forum and practical examples.

Unfortunately, as you'd expect, I won't be able to answer specific excel queries outside of those that relate directly to examples in this book.

Chapter 1 A First Look at Excel 2010

- Spreadsheet – Workbook – Worksheet
- Anatomy of an Excel Workbook
- Open, Save and Close a workbook
- Backstage view
- Info Menu Command
- RECENT menu command
- NEW menu command
- PRINT menu command
- Save & Send menu command
- Help menu command
- Options menu
- Customising the ribbon and Quick Access Toolbar in back stage view

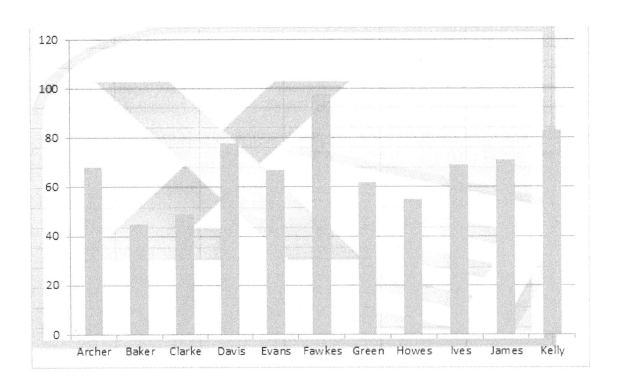

Chapter 1 A First Look at Excel 2010

In this first look we have to tackle an unavoidable subject, Excel is full of jargon that you may not have come across before. The only thing to do is to give you a quick overview and to keep using the terms until you become familiar with them.

On the upside, the jargon is fairly self-explanatory and it doesn't get in the way of creating spreadsheets.

Spreadsheet – Workbook – Worksheet

A spreadsheet is a piece of software for organising and analysing data in a tabular form. Excel is a SPREADSHEET programme.

When you open Excel for the first time, it opens up a blank WORKBOOK. When you save your Excel file, it saves the workbook. By default, your workbook will be made up of three WORKSHEETS (you can change this at any time).

The worksheet is where you will enter your data, perform calculations and produce graphs. When many people think of a spreadsheet, they are really thinking of a worksheet.

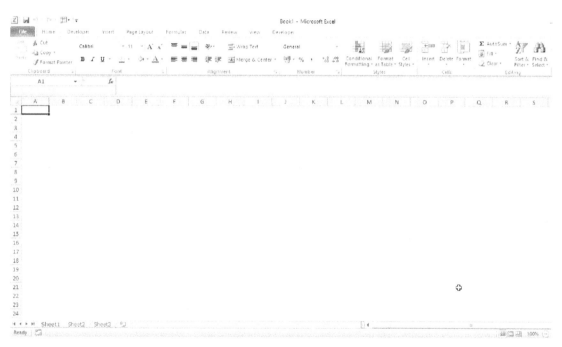

Figure 1 Workbook containing worksheets

In figure 1, you can see an open workbook, with three worksheets.

Anatomy of an Excel Workbook

The bulk of the workbook screen is made up of the PROGRAM WINDOW. In Excel, by default, it is made up of ROWS indicated by increasing numbers, and COLUMNS that are referenced by increasing letters.

The table is made up of individual CELLS. These cells can be referenced by a column then row reference. For example C2 means go to column C and then go down to row 2. You can think of it as being like a map reference.

A cell can contain different types of DATA. This could be a number, text, date, currency and several others which you will be introduced to during the course of this text.

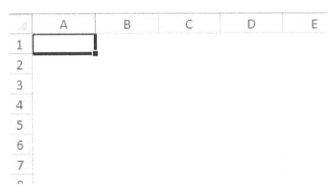

Figure 2 Program window

If you are a new user of spreadsheets, it can be handy to think of cells as being individual boxes that you put your data in. The highlighted cell in figure 2 is at A1.

Above the program window is the RIBBON. This was first introduced in Excel 2007; previously there were just MENUS and MENU COMMANDS. When first transitioning from an earlier version of Excel to 2010, using the ribbon can be confusing. However, it very quickly becomes intuitive.

The ribbon is where you find all the commands and tools that you will want to use. It can be customised.

Figure 3 Ribbon, made up of tabs containing groups

The ribbon is subdivided in to TABS and these are further subdivided in to GROUPS.

Figure 4 Home tab showing clipboard and font groups

Microsoft has tried to bring related commands together so that working with the ribbon quickly becomes very natural. You will be introduced to many of these as the text progresses.

When you have been working with Excel for some time, you may want to bring together commands that you find most useful in one place. This is the QUICK ACCESS TOOLBAR. This is located just above the ribbon, and can be customised.

Figure 5 Quick Access Toolbar

Within each group, you may be able to interact with Excel using a DIALOGUE BOX. You can open the dialogue box by clicking on the DIALOGUE BOX LAUNCHER. Perhaps the best way to describe this is to use one. You can see that there is a FONT group. This allows you to change aspects of the font (type, colour, size etc.). There are many other choices you can make. For this you click on the dialogue box launcher.

Figure 7 Dialogue

box launcher

(highlighted)

The font dialogue box then opens. You can see that you have many more options than appear in the group.

Within the groups are ICONS. These are the buttons or pictures that you click to access GALLERIES and LISTS. Galleries and lists are like dialogue boxes which give you options to use. A gallery is a selection of pictures and a list is as it sounds a list of text to choose from.

Figure 6 Font dialogue box

Figure 9 Cell style galleries

Figure 8 Cell format list

There will be times that you want to zoom in to sections of your worksheet, for example if you want to see more of your work on your screen. There is a handy SLIDER and list that you can use at the bottom right of your screen.

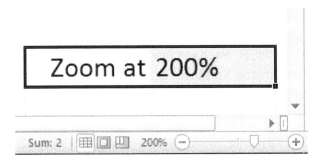

The slider can be controlled either by using the + or − icons or by dragging the control left or right as appropriate.

You can also click once on the zoom amount (100% by default). This brings up a list of predetermined values.

Figure 10 Zoom slider and list

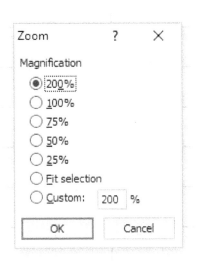

Adjacent to the zoom control are VIEW BUTTONS. These are used to switch between different views (normal, page layout and page break). For now, keep to the normal view.

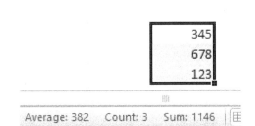

Figure 11 Zoom control list

Figure 12 Status bar showing information

The grey bar at the bottom of the Excel Window is the STATUS BAR. It provides handy information about the worksheet or cells that you have highlighted. In the example a small series of numbers have been selected and in this instance the status bar counts how many cells have been selected, what their average and total values are, without the aid of any formulas.

Open, Save and Close a workbook

In this section you will see how to open, save and close a workbook. You will also see how to open more than one workbook at a time, how to close workbooks and to close Excel.

To OPEN Excel, **double click** the icon on your desktop. A double click is what it says on the tin, you click twice. If you don't have an icon already on your desktop, you will be able to find Excel through your start menu.

This will open a blank workbook, as you have already seen in Figure 1.

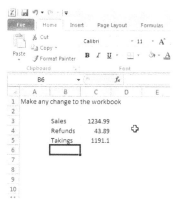

Make some changes to this blank workbook. In this instance you should add some text and some numbers. For the purpose of this exercise it isn't important what these changes are.

Click on the FILE TAB at the top left hand side of your screen. This is where you will access Office file commands. This tab will be explained in more detail in another clip

Click on SAVE. This does exactly what you would expect. It will save your work.

Figure 13 Make some changes

My advice is that you give your file a meaningful name. For example "Sales Figures 2016" is more understandable than "Work Stuff". Oh, and make sure you keep back-ups of your work!

If this is the first time that you are saving this particular workbook, then you will be presented with a SAVE AS DIALOGUE BOX. You can choose where you want to save your file.

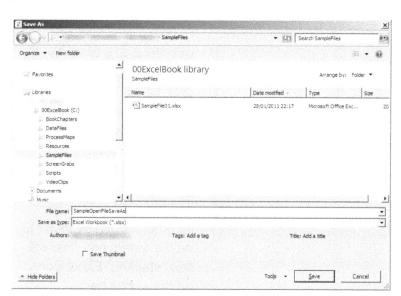

If you are going to be sharing your work with other people who may not be using Excel 2010, then save it as an earlier version which may have the file extension ".xls". If the file is just for you, or everyone is on Excel 2010 then the default save as type is "*.xlsx".

Figure 14 File save as dialogue box

The keyboard short cut to save is Ctrl + S. Keep the control key depressed on your keyboard at the same time press S.

To close the spreadsheet you can either select CLOSE on the file tab.

Or to achieve the same result click the CLOSE WINDOW ICON at the top right of your workbook. This leaves Excel open, but with no open workbooks. You may want to start another spreadsheet.

Figure 15 Close workbook

Figure 16 Close workbook

By selecting the file tab, and selecting close, Excel will close down.

To open a previously saved workbook select the file tab, then select open. Navigate to the file you wish to open and click and then click the OPEN BUTTON at the bottom right hand side of this dialogue box.

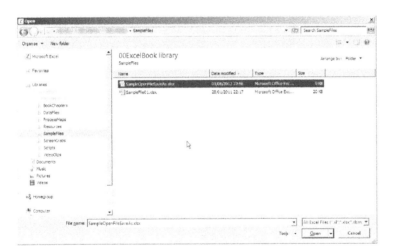

Figure 17 Open existing workbook

You can repeat the process to open more than one workbook at a time. As before FILE OPEN SELECT click OPEN BUTTON. You may want to have several spreadsheets open as you may want to copy information from one to another. You can tell that you have more than one workbook open by looking on the status bar. You will see "stacked" Excel icons on the status bar.

Figure 19 More than one workbook open

Close Excel by clicking on the upper right of your window on the CLOSE ICON.

Figure 18 Close

When you close your workbook, you may be presented with a dialogue box asking if you want to save changes. You options are to either SAVE Don't Save or CANCEL as appropriate.

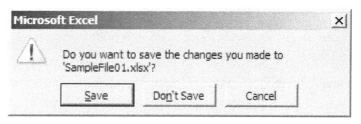

Figure 20 Save - don't save – cancel

Backstage view

The BACKSTAGE VIEW is where you can control what information is saved along with your document, access recent files, printing commands and much more. You can also select which options to activate in Excel.

Figure 21 Click on File tab to get to backstage

To get to the backstage view, click on the File tab.

This is quite a busy tab, and you will look at parts of this in more detail shortly. Note that when you click on a command in the menu, the right hand side of the view changes.

The first commands in the menu are SAVE, SAVE AS, OPEN and CLOSE.

You can use other ways of using these commands. For example, you may click on the floppy disk icon, or use the keyboard

Figure 22 Backstage view Info

command Ctrl + S to save your file.

You've already seen how to open, save and close files. The actions are identical when used from the backstage view.

You will investigate each of these menu items in turn and see how to use them. As a matter of good practice, you may want to make some changes before you start work on your spreadsheet.

Info Menu Command

It may come as a surprise to some users, just how much information about the spreadsheet is kept along with the document. All of it serves a purpose, but you may want, or need to, change some of it to suit your personal or company policies.

The backstage view is in three parts. The menu is on the left, the information and buttons in the middle and on the right, a preview of the properties.

This preview outlines some basic information about the properties of the document, such as file size, dates and related people and documents.

If you work on your own or you don't share spread sheets with others, then much of this is unimportant to you. However, if you collaborate in any way, you may already have used these without knowing. For instance when looking for a document in My Computer, you may have filtered by date created. This screen allows you to make changes, such as adding a TAG or adding a COMMENT.

You use a tag to add details that are important and closely related to the workbook. Changing a tag is not necessary for single users, but is very important if you use a tool such as SharePoint at work. It helps with searching.

For now, click on the "show all properties" link and note how the right hand side has changed.

Figure 23 Change tag details

When working collaboratively, it may be important to give credit to co-workers, or to categorise the document as "draft" for instance. Edit as many or as few of these properties as appropriate.

Properties ▾

Size	19.7KB
Title	This is Sample File 01
Tags	File Tab
Comments	By clicking on the greyed out text, you are able to edit the contents for that field|
Template	
Status	Add text
Categories	Add a category
Subject	Specify the subject

Figure 24 Add a caption in properties

The central part of this screen is where we change permissions, prepare for sharing and manage versions of our document.

If you have created a spreadsheet for your own use, and are not using it on more than one computer, it is most unlikely you will change permissions.

However, if you have created a spread sheet for colleagues to use, such as a conversion calculator or time sheet, you may not want them to alter formulas or enter data anywhere other than specific cells. This is where permissions are so important. You will return to this later in the text.

Figure 25 Protect workbook

Figure 26 Permissions - Prepare for sharing – Versions

You can encrypt the workbook with a password. Click on the "Encrypt with Password" icon. You are then prompted for a password, and then again to re-enter this password. This is to make sure that we have entered it correctly. If you forget your password, it is almost impossible to open your document.

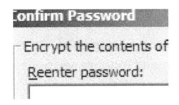

Figure 27 Re-enter the
password to confirm

Figure 28 Enter a password

You can see once your document is password protected, the permissions space is shaded.

When choosing a password, don't use something obvious such as names of children or pets. For simple security you should use a mixture of letters and numbers.

Figure 29 Prepare for sharing

If you are sharing your document with others you need to understand that it contains more data than just what you see on screen. It will contain comments, author details and dates. It may also not be in a format that some people with disabilities would be able to read.

Figure 30 Inspect document prior

By clicking on the Check For Issues icon, you will be presented with a series of choices. The first is to inspect the document.

This dialogue box enables you to check for issues you may be concerned about.

There are several reasons to check your document. You may have aide-memoire in our comments that you may wish to keep private; similarly you may not wish to share personal information. You might have hidden column, rows or worksheets that contain proprietary information. By clicking the Inspect button, Excel will alert you to anything you may wish to change before sharing.

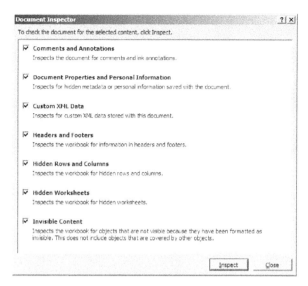

Figure 31 Document inspector

This report will enable you to decide what you want to remove and what you don't. Unselect the content you do not wish to be checked.

Clicking the remove all button will remove those elements you wish to change. You can also go in to your document and remove any details of concern manually. It is good practice to re-inspect your document to ensure you have removed everything that you need to.

When a file is closed without being saved, it is auto saved. The Manage Versions command assists the user with finding this auto saved file.

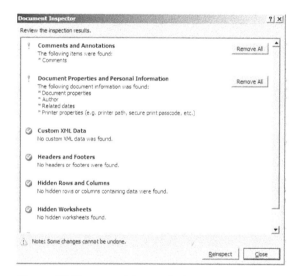

Figure 32 Document inspected

Click the icon and it will attempt to recover any unsaved workbook.

Figure 33 Version - recover unsaved workbook

If there are any unsaved files, the Open File Dialogue box will take you to your default location.

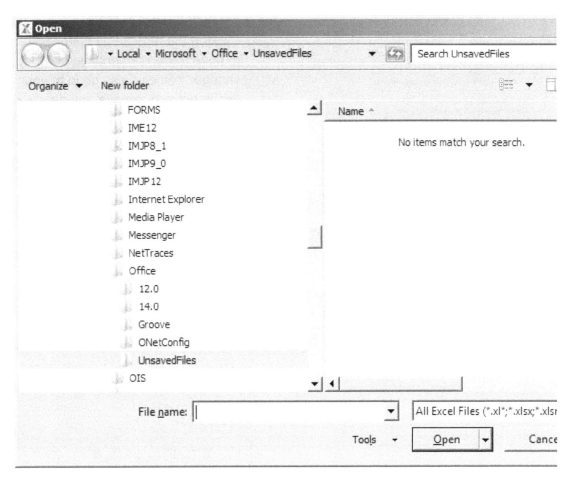

Figure 34 Unsaved files - default locations

RECENT menu command

This is rather self-explanatory, in that it enables you to see your most recently used Excel spreadsheets. Click on the Recent menu command.

There are also three elements to this screen. On the left there are the available commands. In the centre you can see the most recent files that have been opened by Excel. On the right, there are the most recent directories that have been accessed.

Figure 35 Recent menu command

Figure 36 The full recent files screen

You can specify how many worksheets you wish to have quick access to on the left hand side of the screen.

Figure 37 Change the number of recent files to view

Here you can specify how many worksheets you want available on the left of the screen. The maximum is 25. This is a big improvement on Excel 2003, where you could see only 9 spreadsheets. If you set this to zero, then no work books will appear here.

As with many things Microsoft, there is more than one way to do the same task. In this instance, by unchecking this box, the number of quickly accessed workbooks is set to zero.

You may want to keep a number of files in the recent workbooks section regardless of how long it is since you have opened that file. This is where you pin to the recent file list. You do this by clicking the pin icon. The file shortcut is kept even if you clear the recent file list.

Figure 38 Set recent files to zero by unchecking

This is a very handy way of accessing files you frequently use. A lot of Windows users will save their files to Desktop, which creates an icon and clutters their front screen. This is a far more practical and tidy way to get to files.

The pin has turned blue and has moved the file to the top of the list. You can change the position of the pinned file by clicking and dragging. You can also pin recent places.

Figure 39 Pin recent files

To clear the unpinned workbooks, right click one of the listed workbooks to see the options available. You can remove individual workbooks or remove all unpinned workbooks. If no workbooks are pinned, then all will be cleared. The same technique works in recent places.

Figure 40 Remove from pinned list

Figure 41 Files pinned to recent documents list

NEW menu command

Creating a new workbook couldn't be easier. Simply click on the File tab, then New and then…. You are presented with an awful lot of choice!

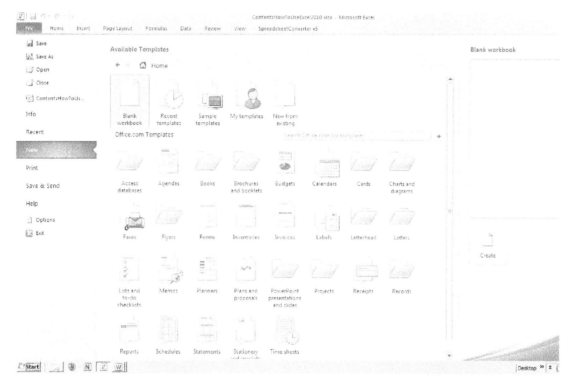

Figure 42 Excel templates

This screen shows you templates which can help you create a new document. In many cases, you want to start off by creating your own workbook based on the BLANK TEMPLATE. You will look at creating your own templates another time. For now we will just double click blank document (or click on the CREATE icon).

A new workbook is created based on your NORMAL template. Before you start working on your new spreadsheet remember to Save As. Then you can make as many changes as you like.

Microsoft have retained their KEYBOARD COMMANDS from earlier versions of Excel. To open a new blank workbook, you can just click Ctrl-N.

Figure 43 Rename default tabs

When you open a new spreadsheet, Excel is set up to create three worksheets in the workbook. You can change this to suit. You can rename worksheets from the default title of "Sheet 1" etc. You do this by right clicking on the tab to be renamed, and then over type with the new name.

You can do this to as many worksheets as you need to. By clicking on the tabs at the bottom of your workbook you can move between worksheets.

Figure 44 Rename additional tabs

Figure 45 Insert additional worksheets

You can add additional worksheets as required by clicking on the Insert Worksheet icon at the right of the named tabs. The keyboard short cut is Shift +F11.

You may wish to reorder your worksheets. You can achieve this by clicking and holding on a tab, and then drag it to the new location in your workbook.

Figure 46 Move tab order

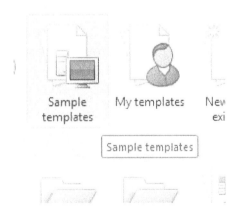

Figure 47 Use a sample template

There are some pre-prepared templates Microsoft has included with the basic installation. To see what is available click on the Sample Templates icon.

There are plenty to get you started. To show you how useful templates can be you will select the Personal Monthly Budget.

Figure 48 Personal Monthly Budget template

Click on the Create button (or double click on the icon) and a new blank personal monthly budget is created ready to be customised and filled in.

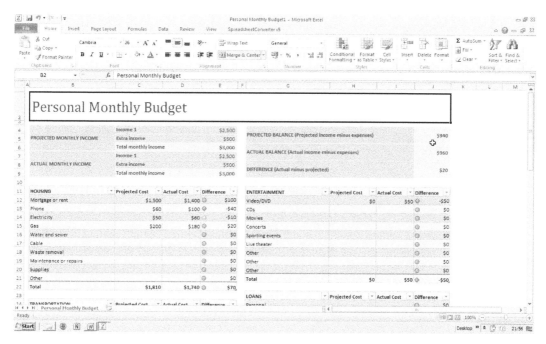

Figure 49 Created file ready for editing

As with the blank spreadsheet earlier, you should File Save As before you start to enter data. This template has columns and rows set up, cells ready for information and some basic formatting. This particular spreadsheet has been set up for $ but it can easily be changed to £ or any other currency.

If you have access to the internet, Microsoft has created links to additional templates that are available from microsoft.com. Take a good look around here to see if there is an existing template that you can adapt. This may save you lots of time on any of your projects.

PRINT menu command

Figure 50 PRINT icon in backstage view

You will now look at the basics of printing. As there are so many printers available in the market place, we couldn't possibly cover every single option. You may only have your home printer to use; others will have a range of printers across a network. To help with printer set up it may help if you can find your printer manual.

Printing can get complicated as you don't actually have to print to a physical printer. You can print to a file, create an xps file or print to a programme like MS One Note. You will see what these options mean in this section.

You can see from the screenshot below that I have one physical printer connected to my machine, a handy PDF creator and also XPS and OneNote as print options.

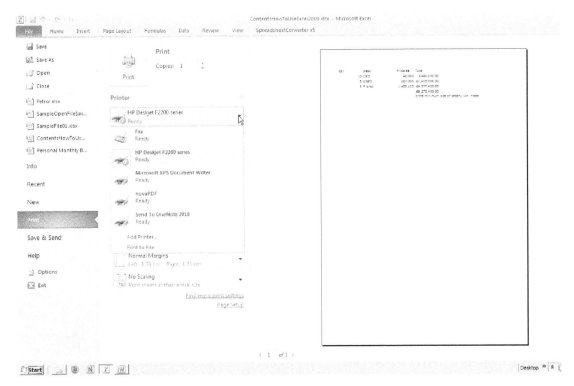

Figure 51 List of printers

There is also a Print Preview on the right of the window. The keyboard command Ctrl + P brings you to this screen.

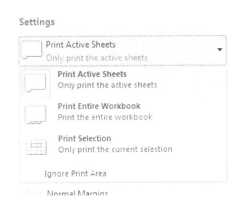

Figure 52 Print options

Excel offers several options for printing. Usually, you will only want to print the active sheet, and this is the default. However Excel enables you to also print the entire workbook or just a highlighted selection.

Often, particularly in a larger spreadsheet you have created, you may just want to print a selected area. To do this, select your choice of cells, and then choose print selection.

You can also define your print area by selecting the Page Layout tab, and clicking Set Print Area.

It can be very useful to save a spreadsheet as an XPS file (technically this is an XML Paper Specification). This is a file type that can be opened by all modern versions of Windows. It can be used when you are away from your base and need to print a document. Then when you are next connected to your regular printer you can simply print the XPS file you have created.

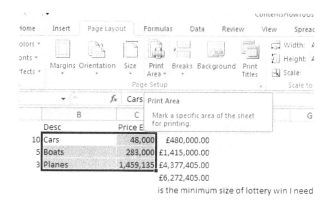

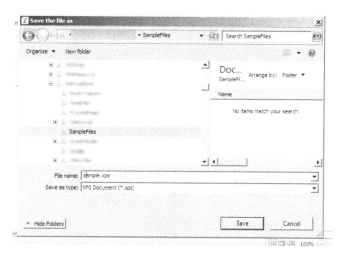

Figure 53 Set print area

Figure 54 Save as XPS file type

Save & Send menu command

The save and send screen can appear to be quite complicated. The first thing to note is that there are several ways in which your file may be saved, and several ways in which you might want to share it or send it.

For example, you may want to send as an email attachment using your default email. You then have the choice of this being a copy of the original document, an XPS or PDF copy or even as an internet fax, if you have this set up.

You have options as to where you send it to. You can publish to the web or to SharePoint if you have an appropriate SharePoint account.

I have Outlook set up as my default email client. Clicking Send as an Attachment attaches the file to a new email.

An alternative could be to open up your favourite email application and then attach the file.

The send as PDF and send as XPS is almost identical. The advantage of sending in either of these formats is that it is difficult for recipients to alter the files that you send them.

Figure 55 Save & Send screen

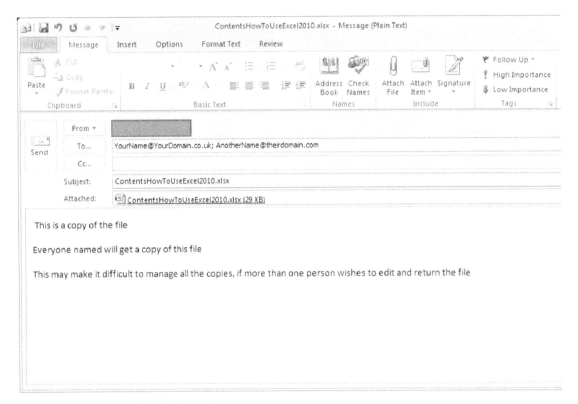

Figure 57 Send as a file attachment

There is an option to Save To Web. This links to your Microsoft OneDrive (previously known as SkyDrive) account. If you don't have an account it is easy to sign up for one. Amongst other things, this cloud based storage allows you to access your files from anywhere with an internet connection. You can even share files with other appropriately authorised users.

Figure 56 Save to web

If you have access to a SharePoint site you are able to save your file directly. SharePoint is a collaborative tool from Microsoft.

Figure 58 Change file type

There is an option to Change the file type. The options presented include as Excel 97 - 2003, template and other file types such as CSV and TXT. You generally would want to do this to maintain compatibility with other systems. For many of these file types it will strip out much of the functionality from the Windows 2010. Of course this can be useful particularly if you are sharing your file with people that don't yet have Excel 2010.

However, I would prefer to save a copy (giving a different name) using the File Save As we saw earlier. That way I keep my copy in the version that I like to use.

By clicking on the Create PDF/XPS icon you will be presented with a dialogue box where you can chose PDF or XPS, and where you want to save your file. This works in exactly the same way as File Save As. These file formats are very useful if you want to save a copy that cannot be easily edited when published.

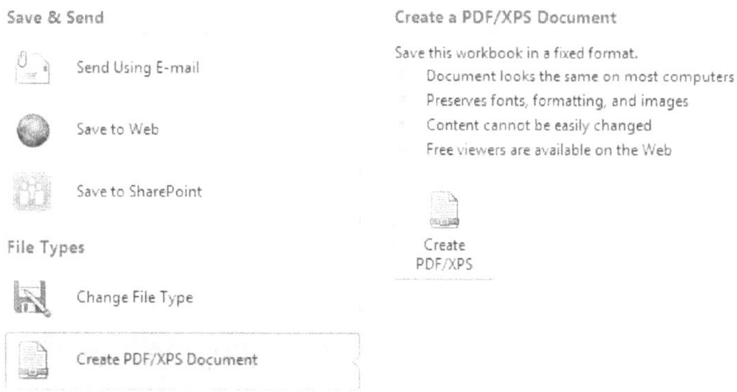

Figure 59 Create PDF / XPS

If you have an account with an internet fax provider, you can send your spreadsheet as a fax directly from Excel.

Help menu command

In my biased opinion the best place to learn about Excel is in this book and by visiting www.practicalexcel2010.com. That said, Microsoft have an excellent suite of help files. You generally have to be online to have access to them all. You can access this from the backstage view by clicking on the Microsoft Help icon. You can also access help by using the F1 key or by clicking on the ? icon at the top right of the workbook.

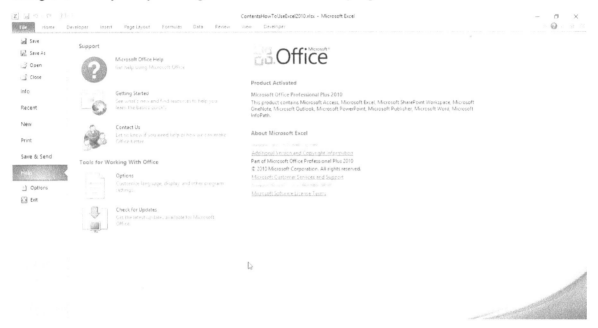

Figure 60 Help menu command in Back stage view

The dialogue box presents you with the options for browsing to a number of help pages such as "Getting Help" or to search for a particular topic.

For example in the top search box type "SUM function" and you will see a number of resources that are available for that particular topic.

This works as if you had searched using the internet. In fact the resources that are brought up are not necessarily those from Microsoft, nor are they all particularly relevant. In this example the fourth and fifth suggestions are for different functions all together!

Figure 61 Help dialogue box

Options menu

There are many different options that you can choose to set. Many people will leave the default settings as they are. There are plenty of good reasons for this, not least that Microsoft have spent time understanding what most users want from the start. However,

there are plenty who have a genuine need to change the standard settings.

It is always good practice to note what changes you have made so that you can roll back if you need to.

Figure 62 Result of searching help on SUM function

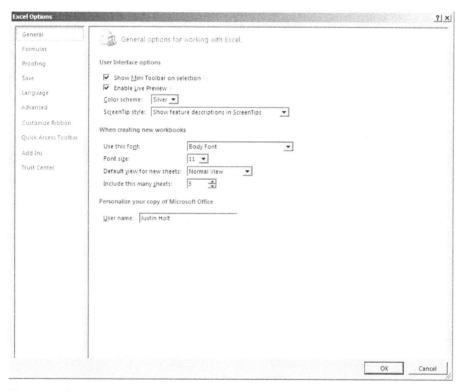

Figure 63 Options in Excel

There are far too many options that you can change to cover in a book of this type. You may wish to take a look and experiment. I will mention some common changes you may wish to consider.

In Formulas – Calculation options – you can see that the default is for automatic calculations. However, you may wish to have Excel calculate only when you want it to, perhaps if you have changes to make and it is a large or complex spreadsheet.

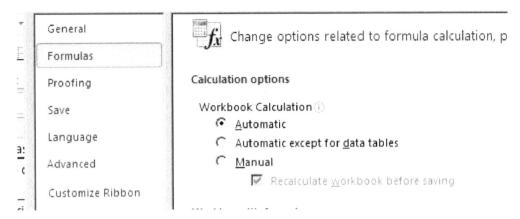

Figure 64 Option - change when formulas are calculated

There are some proofing options you may want to consider changing. For example ignoring words in UPPER case and how Excel handles Auto Correct.

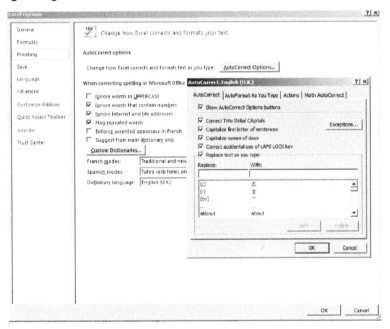

Figure 65 Options – proofing

There are good reasons you may want to change SAVE. You can change how often auto recover information is saved or even the default format. This would be particularly useful if you are working in an environment where not everyone has Excel 2010. You could have it save files as Excel 97-2003 by default.

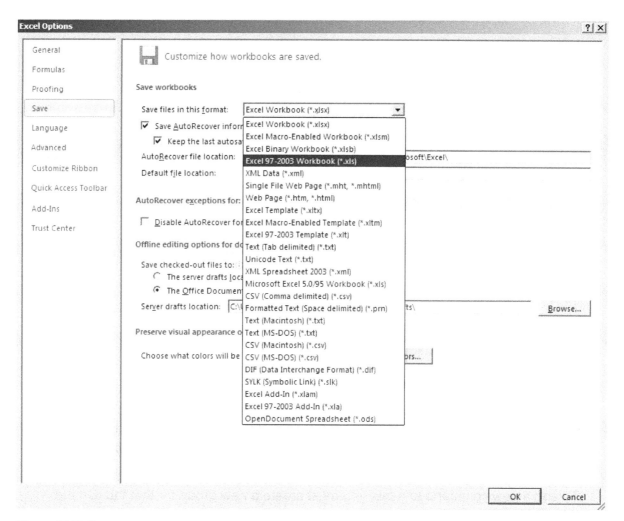

Figure 66 Options – save

Customising the ribbon & Quick Access Toolbar in back stage view

For users that have come to Excel 2010 from Excel 2003, the ribbon may come as a bit of a shock. Everything looks different and isn't quite where you'd expect it to be. To make using Excel easier, you can customise the ribbon.

Selecting File to access the Backstage View, and then choosing Options will provide a menu to pick from. Select CUSTOMIZE RIBBON and you will see a complex dialogue box.

Figure 67 Customise the Ribbon

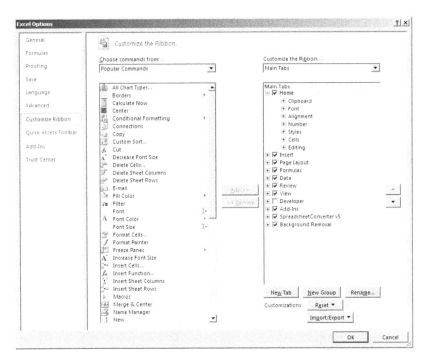

Figure 68 Customise ribbon dialogue box

There a many options that you can chose to add or remove from your ribbon. At this point we will only look at one by way of example. Your instance of Excel may appear differently to the one illustrated here. The principals are the same; you can add and delete any command on the ribbon.

To add a new command to a tab, you must create a new group for that tab. On the REVIEW TAB, you will now create a new group. You can give this any name that you wish, but for this exercise call it My Printing. You can see that it does not exist yet.

Figure 69 Review tab - before customising

First in the backstage view, select options then customize ribbon. On the right hand side, you can see that there is a listing of the tabs and groups that exist in your Excel. Select "Review". Click on NEW GROUP and a new group appears.

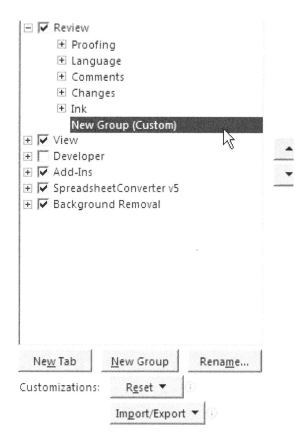

Figure 70 Insert New Group

A dialogue box appears giving you the option of renaming your new group. For this example call it My Printing. You can also assign an icon to the group. In this instance, select the icon that looks like a printer. Click OK.

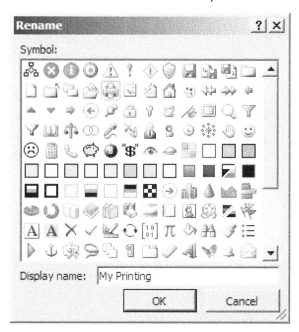

Figure 71 Rename group and choose an icon

Select the new custom group My Printing. Then select QUICK PRINT and then click the ADD button.

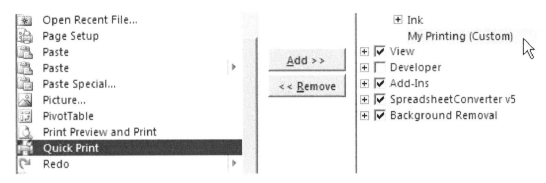

Figure 72 Options - Quick Print

You can see that the Quick Print command has been added to the new My Printing group. Click OK at the bottom of the dialogue box.

Figure 73 Options - quick print added to My Printing group

You can see that the customized group has now appeared on the ribbon and is labelled as My Printing. It shows an icon and title for Quick Print.

This is a useful item to have on your ribbon. You can add more custom groups and more commands in to these.

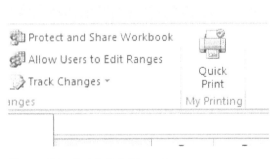

Figure 74 - Quick Print icon in group

If you have a command that you use frequently, you can customise the QUICK ACCESS TOOLBAR. You will have come across this earlier when you reviewed the Excel window. It appears at the top left of your Excel Window.

This is a very handy place to put icons to your most used commands. For instance, rather than change to the Review Tab, and select the My Printing Group and then the Quick Print icon, you may find it easier to place a copy of the icon also in the Quick Access Tool bar.

Select the down arrow next to the Quick Access Toolbar.

You can see the quick print icon has been added to the Quick Access Toolbar. You can add and delete any commands from here.

Figure 75 Add to the Quick Access Toolbar

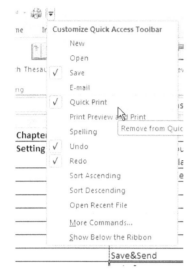

Figure 76 Add Quick Print to quick access toolbar

Select More Commands and then select Borders. Click the Add button.

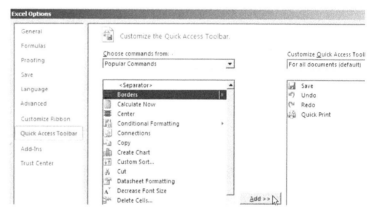

Figure 77 Add borders to quick access toolbar

You can now see that the Quick Access Toolbar has been customised. In this instance with Quick Print and with Add Borders.

Figure 78 Customised quick access toolbar

Chapter 2 Adding Data to Your Spreadsheet

- Making and Correcting Mistakes
- Select Copy Paste Move cell contents
- Selecting cells, columns and rows
- Type of cell contents – formatting as text, numbers and dates
- Other cell contents
- Paste Special
- Find, Find and Replace
- Proofing tools
- Autofill
- Create a custom list
- Using Excel formulas

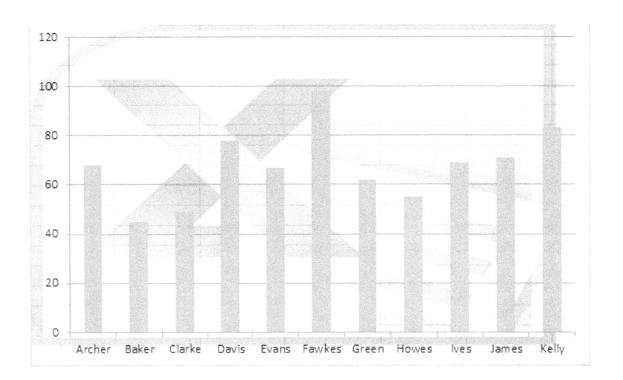

Chapter 2 Adding Data to Your Spreadsheet

In this section you will add some data to your spreadsheet and will see the difference between data labels, values and formulas that are entered in to cells on your spreadsheet.

A LABEL is text that is entered in to a cell. In cell B1 type in the text "Amount" (without the quotation marks). A label gives a descriptive narrative that explains what the figures below are for. In cell A1 is another data label. This is "Month".

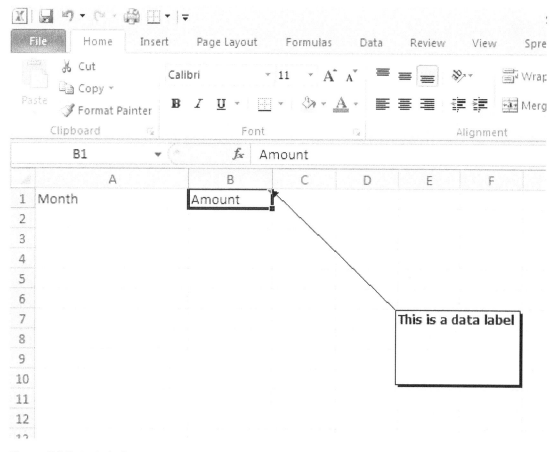

Figure 79 Data Label

Enter the values and labels in figure 80, in to a blank spreadsheet.

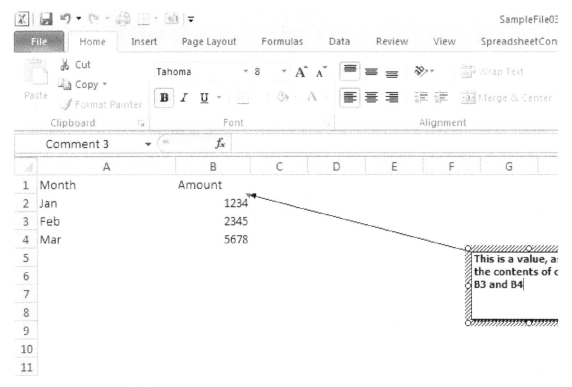

Figure 80 Labels and values

In cells B2 through to B4, enter a series of numbers. These are VALUES.

A value can take many forms, for example it could be an integer (a whole number), a decimal or even a date. One way to decide if the cell content is a value or not is to ask yourself if it could be used in a calculation. If it could be, then it is definitely is a value.

In cells A2:A4, the contents are labels. It makes no sense to subtract the text "Jan" from "Feb". However, if the cells contained dates such as 15/02/12 and say 15/01/12 you could calculate the difference in number of days.

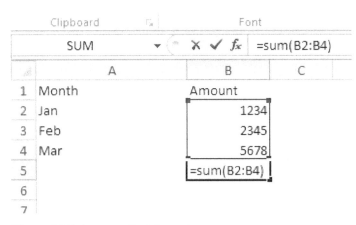

Figure 81 Enter your first formula

In Cell B5, enter the following FORMULA. "=sum(b2:b4)" – do this without the quotation marks. For now, you don't have to know what the formula means. Later you will look at how to construct formulas, which will enable you to turn your data in to useful information. The formula is highlighted in figure 81 for ease of reference.

On hitting enter, the calculation is performed. Cell B5 now displays the answer; The name box gives the cell name; The formula bar shows the formula used.

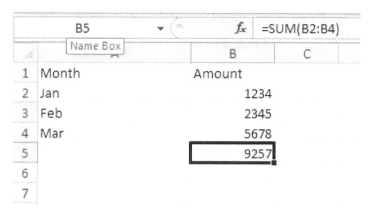

Figure 82 Name box and formula bar

Making and Correcting Mistakes

It is almost inevitable that you will make mistakes when entering data. You can use a keyboard command CTRL+Z to undo the last change you made. To re-do the change you made, you can use the keyboard command CTRL+Y. This keyboard command can be repeated so you can undo several changes. This is a common command in many Windows programs.

However, you may prefer to use the icons provided on the quick access tool bar as standard.

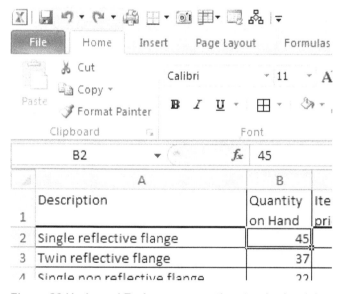

Figure 83 Undo and Redo arrows on the standard quick access toolbar

By clicking on the down arrow adjacent to the undo/redo icons, you can select the specific change you wish to change. It is generally good practice to make your change as soon as you notice you have made a mistake.

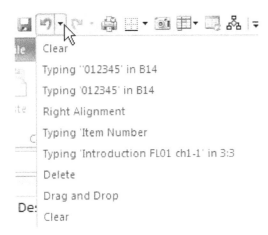

Clear

Typing "012345' in B14

Typing '012345' in B14

Right Alignment

Typing 'Item Number

Typing 'Introduction FL01 ch1-1' in 3:3

Delete

Drag and Drop

Clear

Figure 84 Select which action to undo

There are other times when you may wish to CLEAR your data. The quick way is to just highlight the cell or cells and press the delete button. This isn't always appropriate as you may wish to keep the formatting for example.

The way to achieve this is on the HOME TAB, click the down arrow next to the clear icon in the EDITING gallery.

Here you have the option of clearing all, the formats or the contents. If your cell has comments attached, or contains hyperlinks these can be cleared as well.

You can see the effect of each command in the figures below.

Figure 85 Clear cell contents

Animal	QoH
Cat	2
Dog	5
Rose	22

Clear contents removes the text Rose and 22 from these 2 highlighted cells

Figure 86 Cells to be cleared

Animal	QoH
Cat	2
Dog	5

Figure 87 Clear Contents command

Clear format removes the rose colour

Clear all leaves just blank cells. Had there been formulas in the cell, these would have been cleared as well.

Animal	QoH
Cat	2
Dog	5

Figure 88 Clear Format command

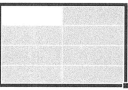

Figure 89 Clear All command

Using the delete button would have kept the formats and just cleared the contents. The effect is the same as clear contents.

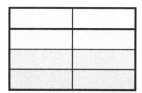

Figure 90 Using delete

Select Copy Paste Move cell contents

In the course of developing a spreadsheet you will inevitably put stuff in the wrong place or wish to make changes to the presentation of where things need to go.

Microsoft has three standard ways to deal with this. You can CUT it from the current location; You can COPY it (this leaves the original contents in place when you PASTE it in to the new location); You can also MOVE it.

These are terms taken from the old days of laying out print. You actually had to physically cut the piece from the paper, and glue it in to its new location. Copy and move are pretty much self-explanatory.

	A	B	C	D	E	F	G	H	I
1	Month	Amount							
2	Jan	1234							
3	Feb	2345							
4	Mar	5678							
5		9257							
6									
7	Cut	Removing the contents of a cell - you can paste when being moved							
8	Copy	Copying the contents of a cell - there is a copy in the original location and in the new l							
9	Paste	The act of dropping the cell contents in to a different place							
10	Move	Moving the cell contents from one place to another.							
11									

Figure 91 Cut Copy Paste Move

There is more than one way to carry out these actions. If you've not had to do these before, they can seem confusing at first. Once you've had a little practice, it will become second nature.

To try these techniques for yourself, create a new spreadsheet with the following details (it does not matter if the contents are exactly those suggested).

Cell Reference	Contents	Format
A1	Month	Text
A2	Jan	Text
A3	Feb	Text
A4	Mar	Text
B1	Amount	Text
B2	1234	Number – no decimal
B3	2345	Number – no decimal
B4	5678	Number – no decimal
B5	=sum(B2:B4)	Formula – number
A6		
A7	Cut	Text
A8	Copy	Text
A9	Paste	Text
A10	Move	Text

The first way to demonstrate how to cut is to first select the cell were the data is. In this instance, highlight A7. Using your mouse, select Cut on the home tab. You will notice that cell A7 has little mouse lines on the outside. These are also known as ant lines, as they look like a line of ants.

Then select cell A6 (of course this could be anywhere you want to move you data to). On the home tab, click paste. The contents of A7 will be empty, and will now be in cell A6.

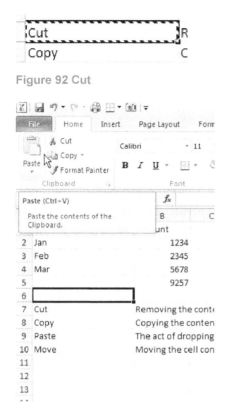

Figure 92 Cut

As you were carrying out these commands you may have noticed that there were some keyboard commands identified when you let the mouse cursor hover over the command. For example to paste, you can see that it says "Paste (Ctrl+V)".

Many people, me included, find using keyboard short cuts to be quicker and more convenient. There are lots available, and remembering a few will help make you more efficient.

You will now reverse the cut and paste, but this time using keyboard commands.

Select cell A6. Using your keyboard hold the Control (CTRL) key down – on my laptop it is at the bottom left; While keeping it held down, hit X. In future a keyboard command like this will be written as Ctrl+X.

You will see the marching ant lines appear around the contents of A6.

Figure 93 Paste

Select cell A7 and then Ctrl+V. You have just cut the contents of A6 and pasted them in to A7 using keyboard commands.

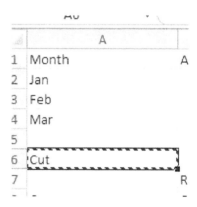

Figure 94 Cut using Ctrl+X

Perhaps the easiest way to move cell contents is to drag and drop. When you select the cell or cells you want to move, the cursor is a thick plus sign.

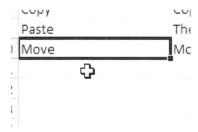

Figure 95 Selected cell with large cursor

When you move your cursor to the edge of the cell or cells, it changes to a four headed arrow. Click and hold the mouse button, and then drag the contents to a new location. It will move when you release the mouse button.

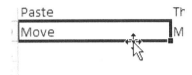

Figure 96 Note cursor changes when you click and drag

Figure 97 Preview paste

You can preview your move by selecting the cell(s) and either using the keyboard command Ctrl+X or by clicking the cut icon, then select the cell where you wish to move your data to, then click on the paste icon. In this example you can see a preview in A12.

A handy short cut is to remember is the undo keyboard short cut Ctrl+Z. If you have moved the data to the wrong place simply use this to undo the move.

You will use this skill many times. It works across Microsoft products. I find the keyboard commands particularly useful, and I am sure you will too.

Copy	Ctrl+C
Cut	Ctrl+X
Paste	Ctrl+V
Undo	Ctrl+Z

Selecting cells, columns and rows

There are many reasons why you would want to select cells, columns and rows and there are several ways to select them.

In this section you will see how to select these individually, more than one, but together (contiguously) and more than one but not together (non-contiguously).

The simplest way to select a single cell is to click on it.

| B6 | ▼ | fx | 12 |

	A	B	C	D
1	Description	Quantity on Hand	Item price	Value of stock on hand
2	Single reflective flange	45	27.89	1255.05
3	Twin reflective flange	37	32.87	1216.19
4	Single non reflective flange	22	19.87	437.14
5	Twin non reflective flange	98	22.44	2199.12
6	Mounted flange	12	102.676	1232.112
7	Unmounted flange	12	89.52	1074.24
8				7413.852
9				

Figure 98 Select a single cell

You may wish to recreate the example in Figure 98 as a new spreadsheet. You can also follow along using any existing spreadsheet you have access to.

In this example, I have clicked on cell B6. Note how the border has changed to show the focus is now on this cell. By clicking on other cells, you can see how the highlight changes as the focus shifts to that cell.

Of course Microsoft provides more than one way to do the same thing. You could enter the cell reference is the Active Cell Address box (aka Name Box). In this case this you can see B6. If you type A6 here, that cell is highlighted.

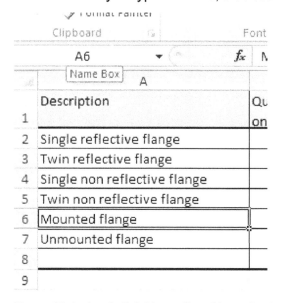

Figure 99 Active Cell Address Box (Name Box)

You may need to highlight more than one cell. If they are next to each other, then click and drag from the one to the next. This can be left to right; right to left, top to bottom and bottom to top.

	Clipboard			Font			Alignm

A1	▼	f_x	Description

	A	B	C	D
1	Description	Quantity on Hand	Item price	Value of stock on hand
2	Single reflective flange	45	27.89	1255.05
3	Twin reflective flange	37	32.87	1216.19

In this example, to select the headers of this small table, click in cell A1 and drag to cell D1. You may wish to do this if for example, you intended to change the formatting. Other ways to achieve the same result would be to select cell A1, and hold the SHIFT key down and then select cell D1. All the cells in between are selected. In the NAME BOX you could also type in A1:D1 to achieve the same result.

You may wish to select more than one set of cells in a row. A common example may be to apply different formats in your table, such as highlighting alternative rows.

	Clipboard			Font			Alignm

G12	▼	f_x	

	A	B	C	D
1	Description	Quantity on Hand	Item price	Value of stock on hand
2	Single reflective flange	45	27.89	1255.05
3	Twin reflective flange	37	32.87	1216.19
4	Single non reflective flange	22	19.87	437.14
5	Twin non reflective flange	98	22.44	2199.12
6	Mounted flange	12	102.67	1232.04
7	Unmounted flange	12	89.52	1074.24
8				7413.78
9				

Figure 100 Selecting more than one cell

In this case you select the first cells A3:D3, then using CTRL key select cells A5:D5. For each set of cells selected, press the CTRL key and select.

This would equally apply if, say, A2:A7 and D2:D7 had to be selected. And also say if you needed cell A2, B3 and any other cell for that matter.

A range of cells can be selected by clicking and dragging. An example where this is particularly helpful is if you wanted to change say, from $ to £ or some other format property.

	C	D	E
y	Item price	Value of stock on hand	
45	$27.89	$1,255.05	
37	$32.87	$1,216.19	
22	$19.87	$437.14	
98	$22.44	$2,199.12	
12	$102.67	$1,232.04	
12	$89.52	$1,074.24	
		7413.78	

Figure 101 Select a contiguous range

As well as clicking and dragging, you could enter C2:D7 in the name range. The key here is to select the top left to bottom right cell that you require.

It is possible to give a name to an individual cell, or a number of cells, and then to use this in calculations or navigation in your spreadsheet. It may be easier for someone to understand the formula " =(CostPrice*QuantityOnHand) ".

You give the cells a name by selecting them, and then typing a name in the NAME BOX. This has to be a single word. So, for example I could select cells A2:A7 and call them ProductNames (but I couldn't call them "Product Names").

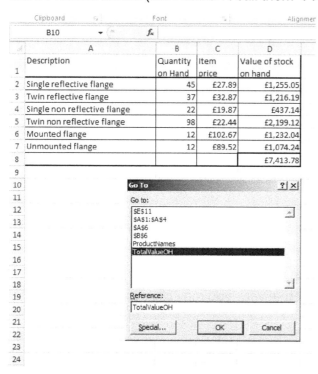

Figure 102 Naming a range of cells

You can then select cells based on the names. To bring up the GO TO box, click on the F5 keyboard button. This is usually on the top row of your keyboard. By clicking on the name you select that range or cell.

Another way of opening this dialogue box is to click on the Find & Select icon on the ribbon, and choose Go To.

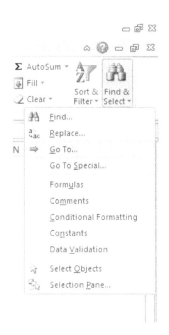

Figure 103 Go To menu command

You may wish to select an entire **row**. You can select the cell in the row you wish to highlight and use the keyboard command SHIFT + Spacebar. Alternatively, you may click on the row number.

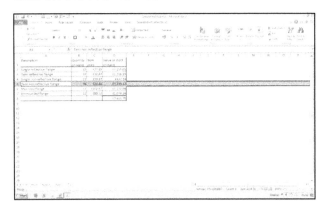

Figure 104 Select the full row

You can select multiple rows by selecting the row, then select another cell then use SHIFT + Spacebar.

Similarly, you can select an entire column. Select a cell in the column and use the keyboard command CTRL + Spacebar. Alternatively, you may click on the column letter.

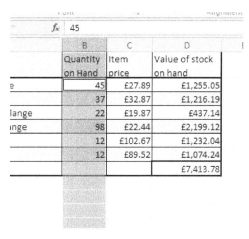

	Quantity on Hand	Item price	Value of stock on hand
e	45	£27.89	£1,255.05
	37	£32.87	£1,216.19
lange	22	£19.87	£437.14
nge	98	£22.44	£2,199.12
	12	£102.67	£1,232.04
	12	£89.52	£1,074.24
			£7,413.78

Figure 105 Select a column

You may wish to select your entire workbook. This is useful if you wish to copy and paste the contents in to a different workbook or programme.

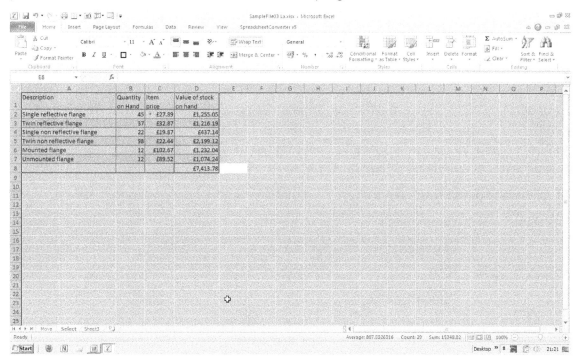

Figure 106 Select All - Ctrl+A

You can simply drag and select as you saw earlier. However, the keyboard command CTRL + A is much simpler.

There are many reasons that you might wish to select cells. It is a very common way to help apply formatting to the selected cells.

It is also very useful to select a range of cells and see the result presented in the status bar.

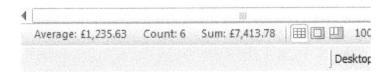

Figure 107 Status bar showing calculations

In the example here, cells D2:D7 are selected. The status bar displays the average, the count and sum in this case. This is very useful to do a quick check without entering a formula in D8.

To choose what is displayed in the status bar. Right click on it and make your selection from the options presented.

Type of cell contents – formatting as text, numbers and dates

The contents of a cell can be formatted in many different ways. What we as people recognise immediately as a number or a date, Excel has to be told exactly how to treat them.

To understand why there are different formats, we must understand what we want to do with the cell contents. For example, we might want to create a list of telephone numbers. It makes sense for these to be formatted as TEXT, as we would never need to multiply two phone numbers together!

To follow along with this example, create a simple spreadsheet of phone numbers.

Cell Reference	Contents	Format
A1	Organisation	Text
A2	BBC	Text
B1	Phone Number	Text
B2	03700 100 222	Text – note the spaces making it easily human readable
A3	BBC	Text
B3	03700100222	General – Note Excel will automatically drop the leading zero
A4	BBC	Text
B4	'03700100222	Note the single quotation mark – this forces Excel to treat the number as text

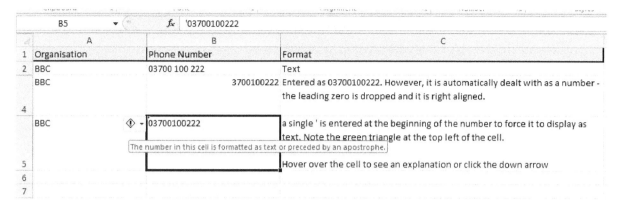

	A	B	C
	B5	▼	f_x '03700100222
1	Organisation	Phone Number	Format
2	BBC	03700 100 222	Text
3	BBC	3700100222	Entered as 03700100222. However, it is automatically dealt with as a number - the leading zero is dropped and it is right aligned.
4	BBC	◇ ▾ 03700100222	a single ' is entered at the beginning of the number to force it to display as text. Note the green triangle at the top left of the cell.
		The number in this cell is formatted as text or preceded by an apostrophe.	
5			Hover over the cell to see an explanation or click the down arrow
6			
7			

Figure 108 Phone numbers are best formatted as text

You can right click on the cell, choose format cell and format this cell to take the "number" and treat it like text.

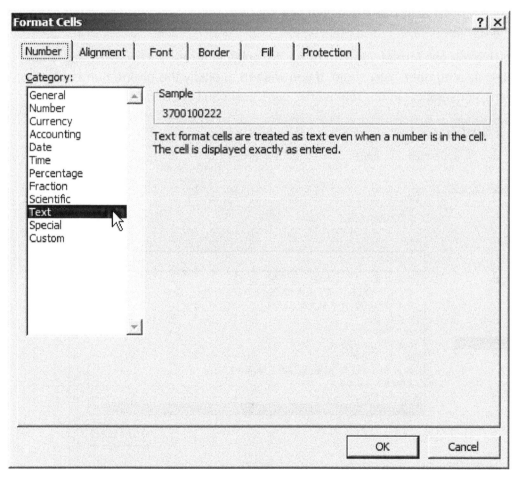

Figure 109 Format as text

You can highlight a group of cells and apply formatting to all of them.

You can also achieve the same result using the Number command on the Home tab. In this case, choosing Text.

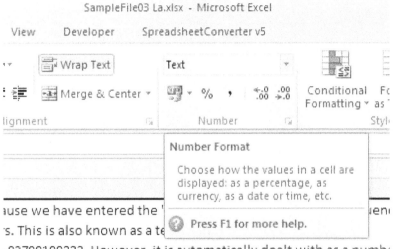

SampleFile03 La.xlsx - Microsoft Excel

View   Developer   SpreadsheetConverter v5

Wrap Text   Text

Merge & Center ▾   %   .00 .00
                                 .00 →.0

                                                    Conditional   Fc
                                                    Formatting ▾   as

lignment   Number   Styl

Number Format

Choose how the values in a cell are
displayed: as a percentage, as
currency, as a date or time, etc.

Press F1 for more help.

ause we have entered the '   uen
s. This is also known as a te
.03700100222. However. it is automatically dealt with as a numbe

Figure 110 Choose Text as a number format

There are quick icons to format the cell to say alter the numbers after the decimal point
or choose currency.

By customising the cell format you can make it display differently. However, this is still
being treated as a number. You could, if you wished, multiply the phone number by two.
This is clearly nonsensical in the real world, but Excel can't second guess this.

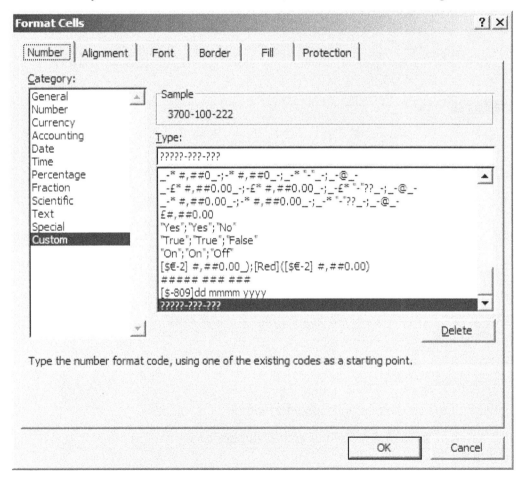

Figure 111 Use a custom number format

In this instance, the format is created in the Format Cell dialogue box, under Custom and I have created the custom format "?????-???-???". In this case, it would appear as text, but actually be a number.

You can display dates in Excel in several ways. It may be that you wish to use a text string. This is fine if no calculations need to be done. However, if you wished to give an expected delivery date as being 10 days after the order date, then it can't be text as you can only calculate using numbers.

Excel thus stores dates and times as numbers. This is an important concept to grasp. To humans it is a date, to Excel it is just another number.

This is a good thing, as Excel can readily do date calculations such as how long to my pensionable date or how much interest is due on a 30 or 31 day month.

The default start date is the first of January 1900. Here in the UK, I would write this the way I describe it- 01/01/1900. This looks the same for North Americans. However they describe the date as January the first 1900. We each know what we mean, we can understand each other, yet we describe the same thing differently.

The second of January illustrates this. I write it as I say it – 02/01/1900. In North America it would appear that I have written February the second 1900.

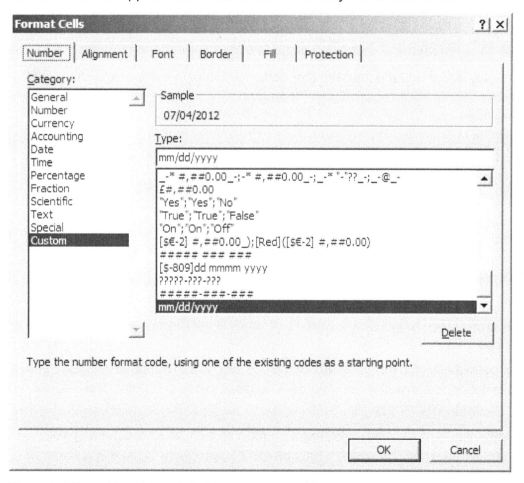

Figure 112 Formatting dates - is it dd-mm-yy or mm-dd-yy

Clearly this could be confusing. You can choose how to format your date in your spreadsheet using dd/mm/yyyy or even mm/dd/yyyy.

This displays the same serial date in a locally understandable manner. There is no "conversion" it is just the format that changes. If you are going to do any calculations, you must be working in the same format.

I can alter this to be a long date format which I choose from the Format Cells Date option.

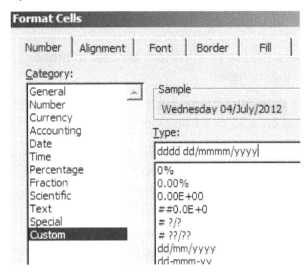

Figure 113 Custom long date format

To display hours, minutes and seconds you could use dd/mm/yyyy hh:mm:ss.

It is easy to play about with the formatting of dates to ensure that they meet the needs of turning your data in to understandable information.

Figure 114 Custom date format to add hours and minutes

The default settings for your locality are usually sufficient for most people.

I can create a custom format to display "Wednesday 04/July/2012". I would use "dddd dd/mmmm/yyyy". For North America, I would use say "dddd mmmm dd yyyy" to give Wednesday July 04 2012".

You can of course alter the format to any of the defaults already created or create your own custom option. For instance you might like to display it as 04/07/12. The custom setting in this case is dd/mm/yy

Numbers can be entered in many different formats. You may enter the number 1000 and it will appear as typed. However, it may be more appropriate to show a number of decimal points.

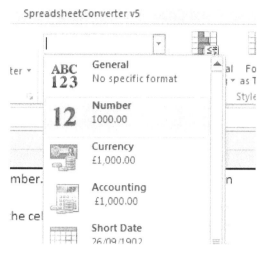

Figure 115 Format numbers to two decimal points

To alter the format, you change it via the Number command on the Home tab.

You may also change it by right clicking the cell, choose Format Cells and Number.

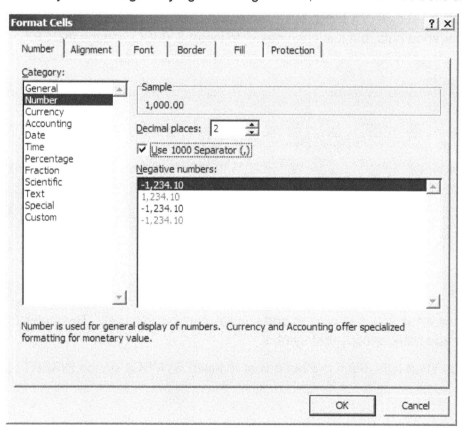

Figure 116 Formatting a number - thousands separator and specified number of decimal points

In this instance, we are display the number as 1,000.00. This dialogue box enables the number of decimal places to be changed to whatever is appropriate to your needs.

You may change the number of decimal points for convenience or to improve display. WARNING: It is very easy to miss rounding errors!!

For example, if you are calculating your personal monthly expenditure then the number of decimal places is unlikely to be important.

However, if you are calculating something that is bought at a price that is set to say four decimal places, yet you only enter it two places then this could lead to significant errors.

NOTE: if you change the display format, the number stays in its original format.

5.7654321 This is shown to seven decimal places

5.77 This is shown to two decimal places

Figure 117 Same number displayed differently

If you were to say sell 6,784,221 units at 5.7654321 the cost to the customer would be 39,113,965.53. However 6,784,221 times 5.77 is 39,144,955.17. This is a difference of 30,989.64. It is always wise to check your results!

Other cell contents

There are occasions when you may wish to add special symbols in to cells. Examples of this could be the trade mark or copyright symbol.

There are character short cuts, but it is often easier to insert SYMBOL on the INSERT tab on the ribbon.

Figure 118 Insert symbol

There are occasions when you may wish to add special symbols in to cells. Examples of this could be the trade mark or copyright symbol.

There are character short cuts, but it is often easier to insert SYMBOL on the INSERT tab on the ribbon.

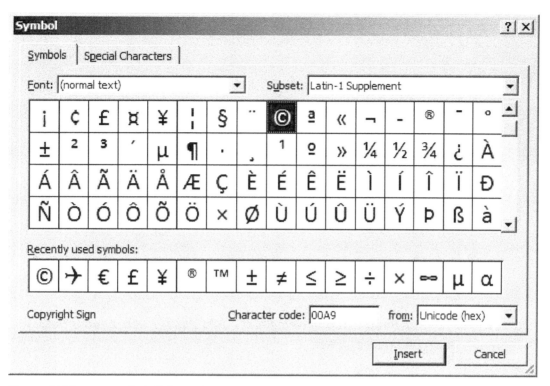

Figure 119 Insert symbol dialogue box

It is sometimes useful to include a link to another document, place in the same document or external website. These links are called HYPERLINKS. If you have ever used the internet, you will already be familiar with these using hyperlinks..

You do this by selecting the cell you wish to have the hyperlink applied to, and then click HYPERLINK on the INSERT tab.

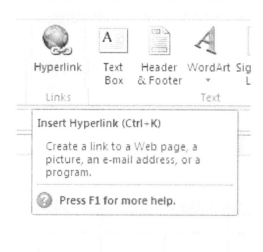

Figure 120 Insert hyperlink

This will give the cell the familiar underlined hyperlink.

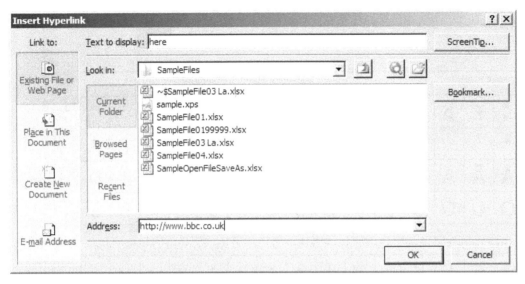

Figure 121 Insert hyperlink dialogue box

In this case, it will take you to an external website. It could equally well, been a place in your document or even an email address.

Paste Special

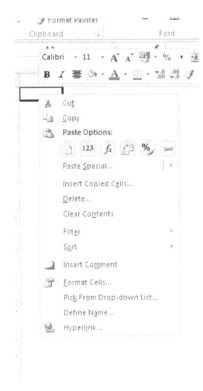

You have already seen how you can paste information that you have copied or cut from elsewhere.

There are occasions where you may wish to do more; this is where Paste Special comes in to its own. Paste special can let you keep formulas rather than just the data; you can just take the contents and not the formula;

When you select a range of cells from a spreadsheet, and then right click to start to paste, you are presented with a list of options. We won't be able to go through every option here, but you are encouraged to "play" and to find out what each option will do.

Figure 122 Paste special options

You saw the table below earlier in the chapter (figure 98). I have copied and pasted it in to a new work sheet. The effect is unflattering.

	A	B	C	D
	Descripti on	Quantity on Hand	Item price	Value of stock on hand
	Single reflectiv e flange	45	£27.89	£1,255.05
	Twin reflectiv e flange	37	£32.87	£1,216.19
	Single non reflectiv e flange	22	£19.87	£437.14
	Twin non reflectiv e flange	98	£22.44	£2,199.12
	Mounted flange	12	£102.67	£1,232.04
	Unmount ed flange	12	£89.52	£1,074.24
				£7,413.78

Figure 123 Paste to an existing worksheet

Below, the option taken was to just paste the contents. Note that it is not formatted for cell colour or for wrapped text.

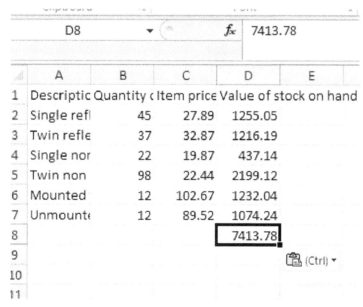

	A	B	C	D	E
1	Descriptic	Quantity (	Item price	Value of stock on hand	
2	Single refl	45	27.89	1255.05	
3	Twin refle	37	32.87	1216.19	
4	Single nor	22	19.87	437.14	
5	Twin non	98	22.44	2199.12	
6	Mounted	12	102.67	1232.04	
7	Unmounte	12	89.52	1074.24	
8				7413.78	
9					
10					
11					

D8   ▼ f_x 7413.78

Figure 124 Contents no formatting

For now note cell D8 containing the VALUE 7413.78.

This is particularly helpful if you want to share the contents of your spreadsheet, but need to keep the formulas secure. You often see this used when figures released to the public.

The next option is to take the table but to include the formulas. Note D8 shows the value 7413.78. However, it contains the FORMULA "=sum (d2:d7)". Other formulas in the copied area are preserved also.

Options:

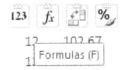

Figure 125 Include formulas

This is useful, particularly if you intend changing the data.

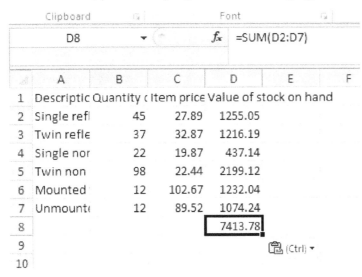

Figure 126 Showing the formula is pasted

It may well be that you have created a worksheet, and want to copy this but not the data.

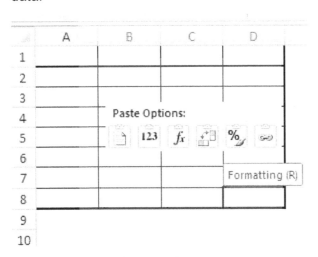

Figure 127 Pasting format only

In this instance you can just copy the formatting.

Paste special includes all the previous options. By clicking on the right arrow you can see some of the other options available.

Note particularly, the TRANSPOSE which turns rows in to columns and vice versa and also the paste as picture. This option is useful to allow end users to see what you are pasting. You would most often use this if you were pasting in to an application other than Excel. You may want to paste a table or a chart in to a Word report you are doing or in to some web design software.

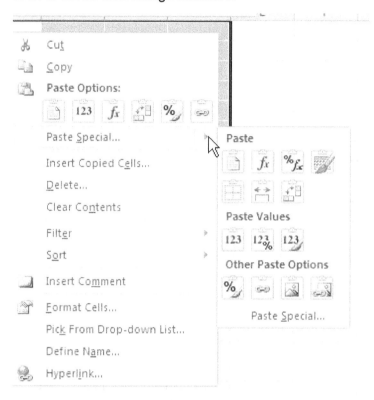

Figure 128 Paste special dialogue box

You can also paste special using the link icon (looks like 3 links in a chain). This means a change in the original source worksheet will be reflected in the final document.

It may seem strange that there is a second Paste Special that you can select. This brings the Paste Special dialogue box. This enables you to do all the actions plus a few more.

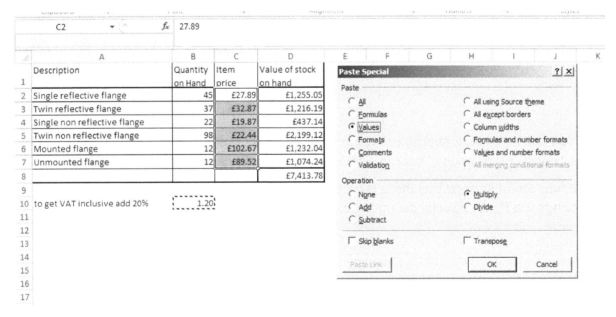

Figure 129 Advanced paste special

As an example, you could apply Value Added Tax (a European sales tax) to the item price, to give a VAT inclusive price to the table.

First enter the rate of tax in a separate cell and copy. Then highlight where the new result is to be applied

Finally, paste special – multiply. To preserve the format of the receiving cells you will need to also click in the values radio button.

| | C2 | ▼ | fx | 27.89 | |

	A	B	C	D	E F G H I J	K
1	Description	Quantity on Hand	Item price	Value of stock on hand		
2	Single reflective flange	45	£27.89	£1,255.05		
3	Twin reflective flange	37	£32.87	£1,216.19		
4	Single non reflective flange	22	£19.87	£437.14		
5	Twin non reflective flange	98	£22.44	£2,199.12		
6	Mounted flange	12	£102.67	£1,232.04		
7	Unmounted flange	12	£89.52	£1,074.24		
8				£7,413.78		
9						
10	to get VAT inclusive add 20%		1.20			
11						

Figure 130 Paste special – Multiply

Find, Find and Replace

As your spreadsheets become larger, you will find that it may be harder to locate information within it. Microsoft provides various ways of finding this information.

We are taking an example of publically available data to use in this example. For our purposes today I have taken the data from http://www.neighbourhood.statistics.gov.uk and thank them for making the information available to the public.

You may wish to take data from the net, or use a larger spreadsheet of your own, to follow along with this example.

Figure 131 Neighbourhood statistics

To get the information, I have highlighted the data on the web page and used the keyboard command Ctrl+C. The curser is placed on a worksheet and then the data pasted as text.

Clearly, this isn't the only way to get data from the web, but it fits our purpose here.

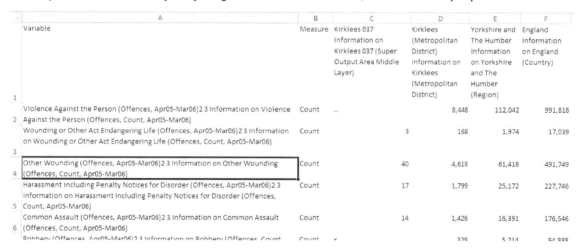

Figure 132 Neighbourhood statistics pasted directly from the web

In the example, look for the words "Other Wounding". In your spreadsheet you may choose to look for another phrase. You can do this by locating Find and Select on the Home tab.

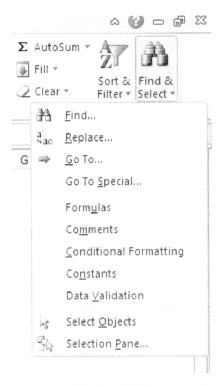

Figure 133 Find and Select menu items

Then click find. In this instance, it finds only one example of Other Wounding. Had the search been on just Wounding, there would have been several other instances.

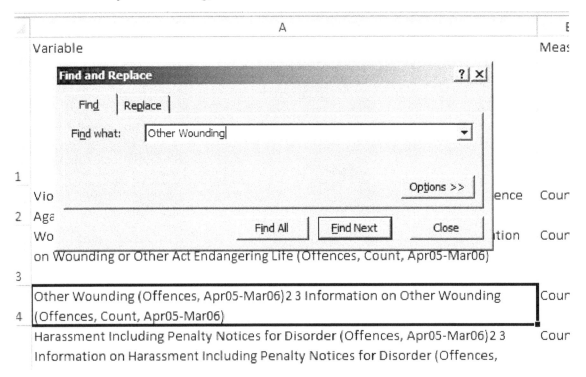

Figure 134 Find - enter your search term

You can search on text, numbers and dates.

Had we wanted to replace the word "wounding" with say "harm" we could find the dialogue box by using the find and search icon on the Home Tab.

You can also use the keyboard command CTRL +F. This brings up the dialogue box you are now familiar with.

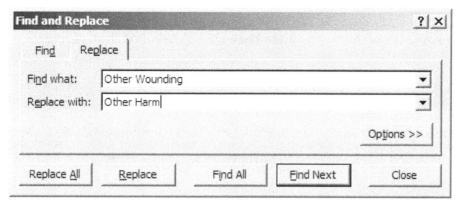

Click on the tab "Replace" and type in to Replace With "Other Harm". You then have the option to replace all instances or just one.

Proofing tools

Correct spelling is one way you can help your data appear to be more professional. As an aid, Excel now has some proofing tools to help. These are found on the Review tab.

The proofing tools are similar to those you will find in your word processor.

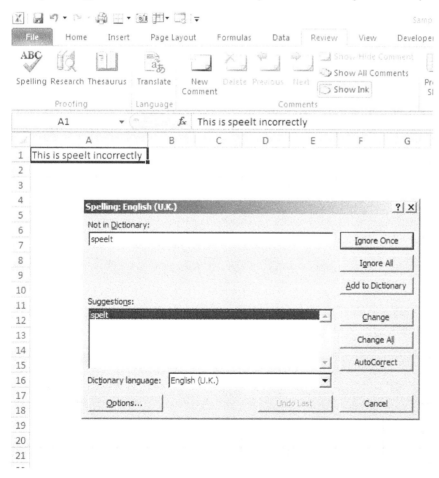

A spread sheet will often have labels that are not in the dictionary. For example you may have cells containing abbreviations such as GDP. You can either add this to your dictionary or you can ignore all that appear.

To check spelling in your spreadsheet, first go to the REVIEW tab, and then click on spelling.

In the dialogue box, you will be presented with the incorrectly spelt word and options to change it, ignore it or to add to your personal dictionary.

You can even choose which language you want to have your spreadsheet checked with.

By clicking on OPTIONS you can select the defaults you need for proofing.

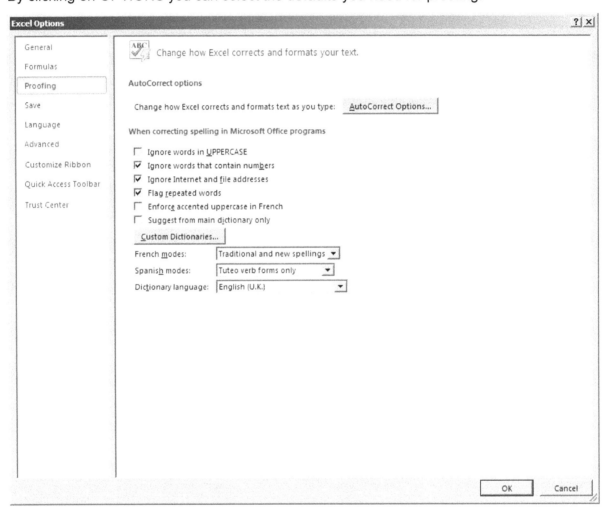

Figure 137 Proofing options

An example may be to ignore words in uppercase if your spreadsheet is a stock control sheet.

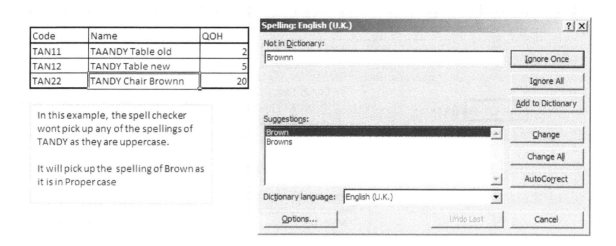

Figure 138 Ignore upper case

In this example, the option has been set to ignore upper case and so it misses the product name but picks up on the colour

Excel has a Thesaurus to help choose similar words.

In this example, the word business may not be appropriate. To use the Thesaurus, highlight the word, go to the review tab, and select from the icon.

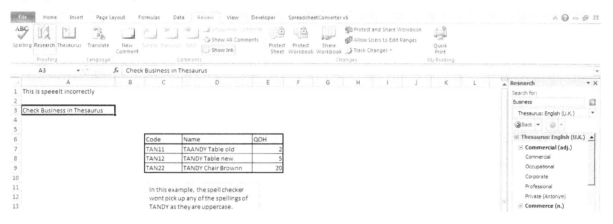

Figure 139 Use Thesaurus

Right clicking will enable you to insert or copy the new word. You will have to highlight and paste in to the correct location.

You can highlight the phrase and choose Research. You are presented with the option to search reference books or use the web.

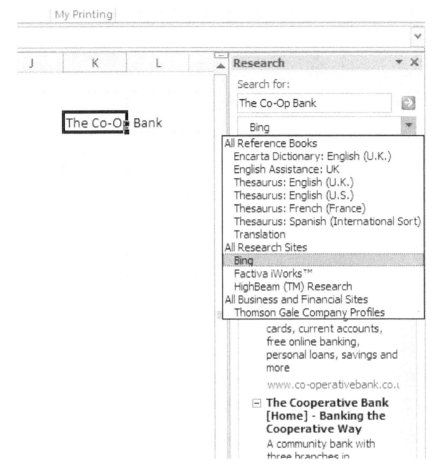

Figure 140 Research

In this example, the search engine BING has been used to present links to appropriate web pages.

There is a Translate option. This should only be used for brief translations, which would result in conveying the idea of what was meant to be communicated.

Figure 141 Translate options

In this respect, no computer can match a human to pick up the nuances of what is meant.

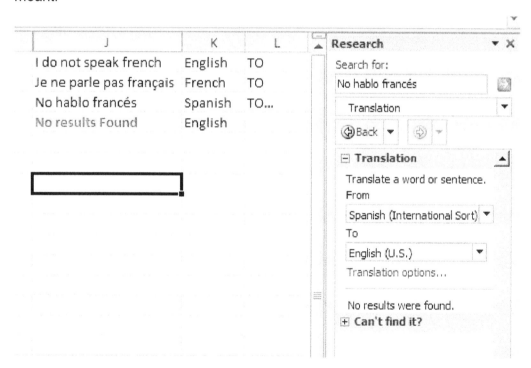

Figure 142 Translated words

In this instance it has proven impossible to translate the result back in to English.

Autofill

Using Excel Auto Fill helps prevent errors and can make data input a little easier.

For example, you can start off a series of cells with text such as Sunday, Monday and then click and drag to complete as many days as is appropriate.

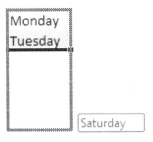

Figure 143 Autofill down days

Autofill works for rows and for columns.

Figure 144 Autofill across days

The technique also works for other data types such as numbers and dates.

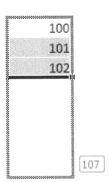

Figure 145 Autofill down numbers

The series doesn't have to increment by one. For example, having the data series starting 100 and 125, the next in the series would be 150, 175 and 200. Clearly the series needs to start with at least two items.

You are able to create a series of your own, even format them, and click and drag these. Auto Fill will continue with the series.

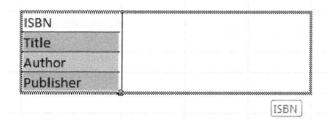

Figure 146 Example of custom autofill with formatting

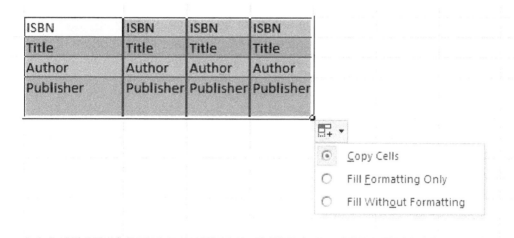

Figure 147 Choosing what to autofill

You can set what you want to have copied, the cells, the formatting only or even without any formatting.

You can set the way that Auto Fill works by clicking on Fill on the Home tab.

Figure 148 Setting autofill options

Excel is smart enough to Auto Fill in series it has not encountered before.

Figure 149 Autofill a non-standard series

Figure 149 Autofill a non-standard series

In this case, we are intending to create a series based on Quarter 1 2015 through to Quarter 4 2017. By entering the first unique set in the sequence, highlighting them and then click and dragging on the Auto Fill Handle (the black square at the bottom right of the highlighted cells) you can drag the series until it is complete.

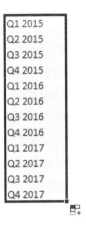

Figure 150 Autofilled non-standard series completed

Create a custom list

It is possible to create your own custom list. In this example you will create a list of hospital wards. Create your list in the spreadsheet (either row or column).

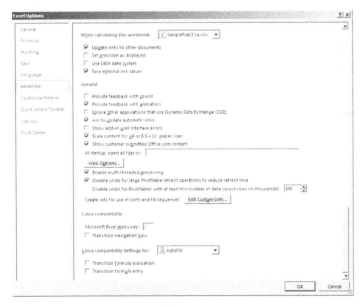

Figure 151 create a custom list

Then on the file tab, click options then Choose ADVANCED and then scroll down until you see EDIT CUSTOM LIST.

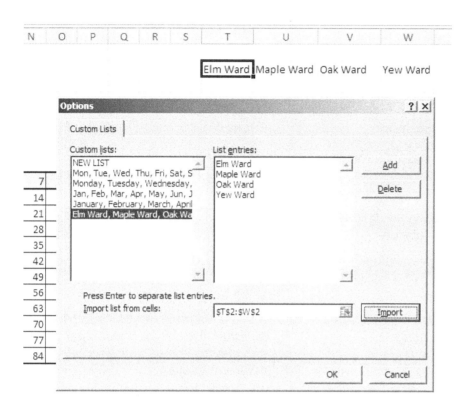

Click Import, then Add then OK. The new list can then be used anywhere.

Using Excel formulas

This has to serve only as an introduction to formulas in Excel. There have been very many books devoted entirely to this subject. My goal is to get you up and running and working with Excel in as short a time as possible and for this to be in the most practical way.

This section will help you understand formulas, what they do and how they can help you with your work. For many new users, formulas can seem daunting. Indeed they can be. I have seen people (often senior managers) reach for their pocket calculators and enter the results from the calculator in to Excel cells!

Be prepared, this is a fairly lengthy section, but once you have worked through it, you will be confident in using formulas.

You will start by looking at simple formulas and then work up to more complicated examples.

Unfortunately you must first understand some of the jargon that is used, and you may find it helpful to refer back here as you gain more experience in Excel. What is important is that you know how to get the result you want and can check they are valid.

A word of caution: Just because your spreadsheet gives an answer, doesn't mean it is right. For example, if your local sales tax is 20% but you entered 22% in your formula, your results will be wrong. It is good practice to check your logic and check your results before you rely on them. That was a fairly trivial example, but we've all heard of NASA's Mars Orbiter that was lost due to conversion problems between metric and imperial measurements, a very expensive and embarrassing mistake.

The table below will describe some important terminology, and then give a plain English example for you.

Term	Description	Example
FORMULA	calculates a result	=SUM(A1:A10) This formula totals the contents of all the cells from A1 through to A10
FUNCTION	built in predefined calculation	COUNT is a function that counts the number of items in a range of cells
CONSTANT	a given value	20% is a constant. You could multiply a cells contents by 20% to get a price inclusive of sales tax
EXPRESSION	A value that is not a constant	A1+B1 You may need to add two cells together. These are not constants as you can change the value in the cells to get different results
OPERATOR	Performs the calculation	+ (plus) – (minus) * (multiply) and / (divide) are operators. There are others
CELL REFERENCE	The location of a cell	Rather like reading a map, there are grid references such as A1 or X67
RELATIVE CELL REFERENCE	When copying or pasting a formula it uses a location relative to where the formula is pasted from	If in cell A4 there is a formula "=SUM(A1:A3)", when copied to A24 it becomes" =SUM(A21:A23)"
ABSOLUTE CELL REFERENCE	Always refers to the contents of that cell, even if copied and pasted or the formula is used elsewhere in your spreadsheet	You may have a multiplier in a spreadsheet, say perhaps an exchange rate (one dollar = 0.76 euros) you may enter 0.76 in cell A27. The absolute cell reference would be written with a $ sign next to the column reference and a $ sign next to the row reference. So this would be $A$27
MIXED CELL REFERENCE	Either the column or row number is fixed	$A1 or A$1
3D CELL REFERENCE	A cell reference across more than one worksheet or workbook. Prefixed with an exclamation mark	=SUM(sheet1:sheet12!B15) This could be used to say total all the results in B15 that are in 12 worksheets.
ARGUMENT	Part of the formula, may be a cell reference or another formula that contributes to the result.	In the formula "=SUM(A1*B7)" A1 and B7 are arguments. In the formula "=COUNT(A1:A5, B1:B5)" then A1:A5 and B1:B5 are the arguments.

PRECEDENCE	The order in which a formula is calculated	If we need to perform the calculation 3+5*7 what is the answer? Depending on the precedence, it is either 56 or 38. It is either 8*7 or 3+35.
		In Excel the rules are that everything in brackets is done first, then working from left to right, multiplication and division are done before addition and subtraction.
		In the UK we use the word brackets to mean "()". Elsewhere they may be referred to as parenthesis or braces. Some people refer to the four in 2^4 as being the order or exponent.
		Thus as a way to remember the order or precedence you could use BODMAS – BEDMAS – PODMAS or PEDMAS. You may remember this from school?
		Excel makes things easy in that you can put brackets in to make the order clearer, or you can use named cells or ranges.

Right now, don't worry too much about these terms. You will encounter them again and their use will become clear.

Also, if you don't think you have used a formula since school, don't be put off. We will be using straightforward examples to start off with.

There are many functions within Excel, and you can create your own. There are financial, trigonomic, scientific, mathematical, text and logical functions. Entire books have been devoted to them. Here we will only use a few to demonstrate how they are used.

Before you get started, I have to repeat some advice I was given many years ago about learning how to programme. A great place to start is to see how other people are doing things. By all means plagiarise formulas within these spreadsheets. I don't mean steal wholesale and claim the work as your own. But if you see a formula that resolves your problem, borrow it, adapt it and share how you tackled the problem. Clearly don't do it with proprietary code, but follow how someone has used the syntax (think of syntax as being the Excel equivalent of grammar) of the formula.

Quantity on Hand	Item price	Value of stock on hand		Formula	Result
45	£27.89	£1,255.05		=D1	Value of stock on hand
37	£32.87	£1,216.19		=B2	45
22	£19.87	£437.14		=D3	£1,216.19
98	£22.44	£2,199.12			

Figure 152 Formula - get the contents of a cell

A formula always starts with the equals sign "=". From now on in these instructions we will omit any quotation marks. If you use them, your formula won't work.

You can enter your formula in the cell or in the formula bar. Probably the simplest formula is one that says put the value in that cell in to this cell here.

The **value** of the cell in the formula also becomes the value in the new cell. To explain, using the example shown, in cell G1, I have entered the formula =D1. The result of the formula is some text. In this case "Value of stock on hand".

If the text in cell D1 is changed to say, "Value SOH" then the result in G1 will change. Try it and see. Similarly, if you change the value of cell B2 from 45 to 54, the value in G3 will change.

You can change the contents of cell B2 to anything you like. It does not have to be a number. In this case change it to be some text. The new contents in B2 are returned as the result in the formula in G3. Note though, this makes the original formula nonsensical. It returns an error message #VALUE!

Quantity on Hand	Item price	Value of SoH		Formula	Result
banana	£27.89	#VALUE!		=D1	Value of SoH
37	£32.87	£1,216.19		=B2	banana

Figure 153 Formula - text where a number is expected generates a #VALUE error

A common use for such a simple formula is where you might want to have a summary of results, either on the same worksheet or in a different workbook. If you change the value in either B4 or C4, the result will change in both D4 and G4.

You can enter your formula either directly in to the cell or in to the formula bar.

Figure 154 Using the formula bar

The formula bar is located under the ribbon, and is adjacent to the name box. It is denoted by the symbol f_x.

The formula bar can be clicked and dragged to increase its size. This is particularly useful when writing nested formulas which you will look at later.

In this next instance you are going to look at ways in which you can calculate the rate of sales tax. In the UK, this is known as VAT and is usually 20%. The way you calculate an additional 20% is to multiply the value by 1.2. This is the same as saying 100% of the original value, plus 20% more. This is only a slightly more complex formula than before. Here, you will be saying "take the value of that cell, and multiply it by the value in the other cell".

	Clipboard		Font			Alignment
E7			f_x	=D7*1.2		

	A	B	C	D	E
7	Unmounted flange	12	£89.52	£1,074.24	£1,289.09
8				£7,413.78	
9					
10	to get VAT inclusive add 20%		1.20		
11					

Figure 155 Include constant in the formula

There are two ways you can enter this formula. The first is to multiply by the direct amount. If you were to enter the formula in E7, =D7*1.2, you are effectively asking what is the VAT inclusive price of the stock on hand. This makes the "1.2" a constant. The big disadvantage is that if the sales tax changed, to say 22%, then you would have to change it in all the formulas.

In many cases, it may be better to enter the value you want to multiply by in a different cell. In this case, the value 1.20 has been entered in to cell B10. If the value of VAT changed, then you would only need to change it in one place and not in all the cells in your spreadsheet.

The formula in E7 would become =(D7*B10).

It is OK to multiply the values in two cells together in a formula such as =D7*B10. However I prefer to use the formula =SUM(D7*B10).

Referring back to the jargon table, =SUM(D7*B10) is the formula, D7 and B10 are the arguments of the function SUM, * is the operator and B10 is a constant.

The reason it is more complete is that by adding the word SUM you are being explicit as to what the formula is to do. In this case sum the two arguments.

When you are developing more complicated formulas, you will find it easier to click on the cells rather than type in say, D7 and B10. You will find you make fewer mistakes that way.

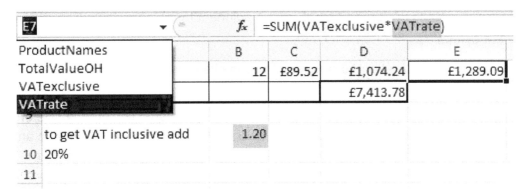

		B	C	D	E
ProductNames					
TotalValueOH		12	£89.52	£1,074.24	£1,289.09
VATexclusive				£7,413.78	
VATrate					
	to get VAT inclusive add	1.20			
10	20%				
11					

E7 — fₓ =SUM(VATexclusive*VATrate)

Figure 156 Name cells or ranges to improve your formulas

It is often better to name the cells (or range of cells) used in a formula. In this example B10 has been named VATrate and D7 has been named VATexclusive. The calculation is far more understandable as =sum(VATexclusive*VATrate) than =sum(D7*B10).

Formula AutoComplete displays when you type the = plus the first few letters of the function you intend to use.

In the example below, looking at the average of the petrol prices in various states, you will see this in action.

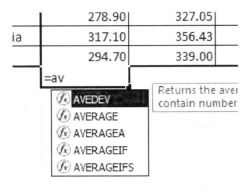

Figure 157 Formula AutoComplete - type =AV and see what appears

In this case, the formula is to =AVERAGE(B16:B25). Referring to the jargon table, Average is the function and B16:B25 is the expression. It means the range of cells from B16 through to B25. In this case, B16:B25 is also the argument of the function.

Regular Price in Cents per US Gallon			N
2007	2008	2009	
271.00	317.20	230.60	
294.10	340.66	246.30	
275.90	317.11	232.60	
276.80	315.44	223.40	
260.60	308.14	216.70	
304.70	350.64	268.60	
286.00	337.66	244.90	
278.90	327.05	236.50	
317.10	356.43	269.00	
294.70	339.00	256.20	
285.98			

Figure 158 The completed formula =AVERAGE(B4:B13)

In the example, the formula is =AVERAGE(B4:B13) and it gives the answer 285.98

This result could be calculated **without** entering a formula. To see this in action, simply highlight the range of cells that you're interested in and look at the status bar.

Average: 285.98   Count: 10   Sum: 2859.80

Figure 159 Status bar can display quick results

If your status bar doesn't display Average, Count and Sum, right click on the status bar and select the quick calculations you want to appear.

This is particularly useful for a quick check of your figures.

It would be arduous and error prone if you had to enter in the formula in to every column you want to calculate.

You can click on the formula in B13 and drag across to J13 and the formulas will be calculated automatically.

317.10	356.43	269.00	325
294.70	339.00	256.20	305
285.98			

Figure 160 Drag your formula across columns

There are plenty of different functions that may be appropriate to use in this context. By way of example, you could choose to look at what the maximum price was for a given range by using the function MAX rather than Average.

You will notice on the ribbon that there is a FORMULAS TAB. To see how to use this highlight a range of cells and then click on the auto sum button.

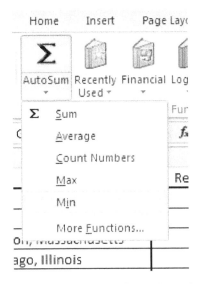

Figure 161 Use the Formulas tab

The answer will appear in the next available adjacent cell.

As an exercise, convert the sales tax exclusive price (in cents per US gallon) in to the VAT inclusive price (in pence per UK gallon).

There isn't an Excel function that has been created to do this. So, you might want to break the task down in to component parts. There are several ways to tackle a problem like this. The method I suggest is to

1. Convert the cents in US gallon to Price in UK gallon (multiplier = 0.833). This is gives a result still in US dollars
2. Convert the result of this to VAT inclusive price (multiplier = 1.2). Again this is still in US dollars
3. Convert the result of this in to UK £ (VAT inclusive) (current multiplier approx. 0.69)

You may prefer to call the multiplier a conversion factor.

Clipboard		Font		A
B32	▼	f_x	=SUM(UStoImperialGallon*B16)	
ProductNames		B	C	D
TotalValueOH	allon	0.833	<< this is a Constant	
UStoImperialGallon				
VATexclusive		2007	2008	2009
VATrate				
31				
32 Boston, Massachusetts		225.74	264.23	192.09
33 Chicago, Illinois		244.99	283.77	205.17
34 Cleveland Ohio		220.02	264.15	102.76

Figure 162 Using a constant and name the cell

You will note as you create your formula that Auto Complete is available and makes completing the formula easier as we have named the cells of the multipliers.

	0.62	<< This is a co
	2007	2008
	=sum(B44*	2409.60
	Doll	380.49
	SUM(number1, [number2], ...)	
	DOLLAR	Converts a num
	DOLLARDE	378.38
	DOLLARFR	369.62
	DollarToPound	
	365.49	420.60
	343.06	405.03

Figure 163 Using named ranges and autocomplete

You can create this either in 3 steps using 2 "helper" formulas to give answers that are used to get to the final stage or you can do it all in one formula. By naming cells you can get a formula such as **=SUM(((D3*USgalToUKgal)*VATrate)*CurrentUSDtoGBP)**.

You will see in the example that there have been three separate operations applied to the original data.

You could have created one single formula and skipped the intermediate steps. However, by following the logic, you can see how the final formula was created. Noting the earlier comments about precedence, you can see that by using brackets, you have ensured that the formula has been derived in the correct order.

| | Font | | | Alignment | | | N |

ƒx =SUM(((B16*UStoImperialGallon)*VATmultiplier)*DollarToPound)

	B	C	D	E	F
	2007	2008	2009	2007	2008
s	167.95	196.59	142.91	175.76	204.62
	182.27	211.13	152.64	189.09	218.14
	170.00	196.53	144.15	177.50	203.10

Figure 164 Nesting calculations in one formula

Using named cells, this is the final formula -

=sum(((B16*UStoImperialGallon)*VATmultiplier)*DollarToPound). If you hadn't used named cells the formula would have been =sum(((B16*0.83)*1.2)*0.62). This would have been harder to amend if the VAT rate or $ exchange rate varied.

This type of formula is described as being NESTED. This means there is one formula, inside another. And in this case, inside yet another. As the formula is being typed, you can see the colour of the text and brackets changes.

This is done so that you can check that for every opening bracket there is a corresponding closing bracket. That means every building block of your formula is complete.

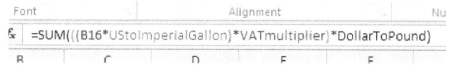

Figure 165 Building up your formula

A message to take away is that Excel is there to do calculations. You have to understand the problem you are trying to solve to be able to create your formula. Break the problem down in to small components an use these to build the final solution to the problem. Naming cells will make it easier for you to understand a formula.

There is an easy way to manage the names that you have given cells or ranges of cells. On the formula tab, click on the Name Manager icon. You will then see this dialogue box which you can create new, edit existing or delete names.

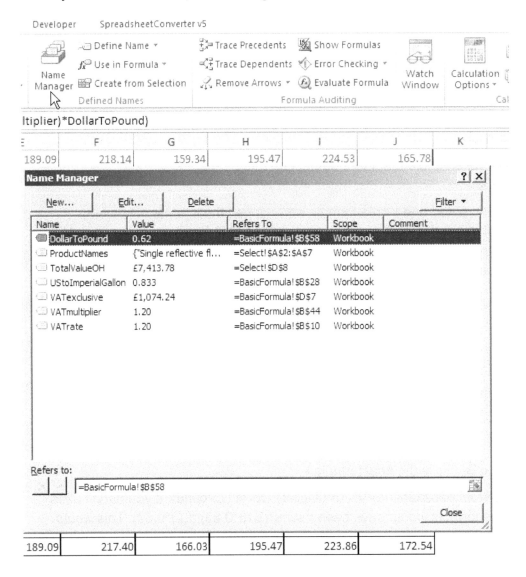

Figure 166 Using Name Manager

It is possible to generate errors when creating formulas.

The difference between

=SUM(((B16*UStoImperialGallon)*VAT   multiplier)*DollarToPound) and
=SUM(((B16*UStoImperialGallon)*VAT multiplier)*DollarToPound)

is not immediately obvious.

In this case, there is an additional space inserted between "VATmultiplier", which in the incorrect formula is "VAT multiplier".

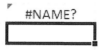

Figure 167 The #Name? error

It is good practice to use a single name, to define your named cell (s). I prefer to capitalise the names as well.

Excel flags up errors and provides a way to assist in correcting them.

When you see a green triangle in the top left hand of a cell, it means there is an error. Click on the cell, and then click on the yellow diamond ! icon that appears and you will be presented with a list of options.

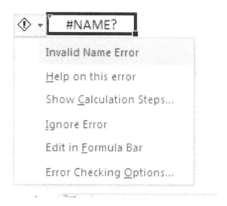

Figure 168 Help with the Invalid Name Error

When you click on the evaluate formula, you will see where Excel trips up. This is your clue to investigate further.

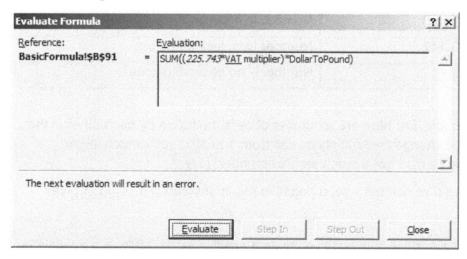

Figure 169 Evaluating the incorrect formula

To illustrate how an error can be identified during creation I have used a formula without enough brackets. =sum(B91*B92)*B93)*B94) The correct formula is =sum(((B91*B92)*B93)*B94) **NOTE:** the formula can be written without the final bracket. I prefer to use them as I know the formula is complete.

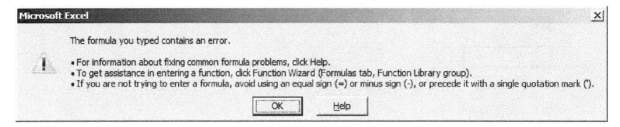

Figure 170 Your formula contains an error

90		
91	First number	226.89
92	Second Number	345.8
93	Pi	3.142
94	Multiply by	1
95	Gives	246516.8018
96		

Figure 171 A simple formula in action

On a blank spreadsheet, create the contents above in figure 171.

Cell Reference	Contents	Format
A1	First number	Text
A2	Second number	Text
A3	Pi	Text
A4	Multiply By	Text – note the spaces making it easily human readable
A5	Gives	Text
B1	226.89	Number to 2 decimal places
B2	345.8	Number to 1 decimal place
B3	3.142	Number to 3 decimal places
B4	1	Number – no decimal places

This is a trivial example. But here are a number of cells multiplied by each other in the formula above. So if change the Multiply by cell from 1 to 10, I get a much larger number. If I multiply by 0.1 I get a much smaller number. (Try it).

If I multiply by a negative number I get a negative result. Instead of 1 using -1 gives

-246516.8018.

The rule is multiply a positive by a positive, gives a positive result. Multiply a positive by a negative gives a negative result.

Multiply a negative by a negative gives a positive result (try it and see).

A special case is when you multiply anything by zero (or even minus zero). The answer is always zero.

At this point, it is important to note that none of these are errors. They are just different results.

.	First number	226.89
!	Second Number	-345.8
:	Pi	3.142
:	Multiply by	0
:	Gives	0

Figure 172 Multiplying by zero isn't an error - it just results in zero

By changing the Multiply By to Divide By and the formula to =SUM((B91*B92)*B93)/B94 we can see some interesting results.

In the first instance, try divide by 1. The result is the same as multiplying by -1. If you remember some school maths this is probably no surprise. In just the same way dividing by -1 is the same as multiplying by +1 (Try it).

Again note that this is not an error.

91	First number	226.89
92	Second Number	-345.8
93	Pi	3.142
94	divide by	1
95	Gives	-246516.8018

Figure 173 Divide by 1

However, to divide by zero IS an error!

There are lots of reasons mathematically, algebraically and computationally as to why. All are outside the scope of this work, but reasonable explanations can be found via your favourite search engine.

Excel flags this by #DIV/0! Again you can click on the "!" icon and can see where the error has occurred and correct the error in either your figures or your formula.

All the Rules

1. Positive x positive = positive
2. Negative x negative = positive
3. Positive x negative = negative
4. Negative x positive = negative
5. There is no rule number 5
6. Positive / positive = positive
7. Negative / negative = positive
8. Positive / negative = negative
9. Negative / positive = negative
10. Anything * zero = zero
11. **Anything / zero = #DIV/0!**

90			
91	First number		226.89
92	Second Number		-345.8
93	Pi		3.142
94	divide by		0
95	Gives	◇	#DIV/0!
96			

Figure 174 Dividing by zero IS an error - #DIV/0!

It makes sense to perform sums only on numbers. Where you try to perform calculations on text, you get an error.

We know that "one" and "two" mean 1 and two. But you can't multiply the text value two by 2. It's just nonsense. And so Excel generates an error.

Figure 175 The #VALUE! error

In the same way click on the ! icon to trace the error if it isn't obvious.

To recap – formulas take some practice but they are easy. There is a lot to them, but Excel really is all about calculations. Keep this section handy as you gain experience.

Chapter 3 Formatting your work

- Page Formatting
- On sheet formatting
- Change row Heights and Column widths
- AutoFit
- Insert Row or Column
- Format Painter
- Delete Row or Column
- Conditional formatting
- Hiding Rows or Columns
- Format as a Table

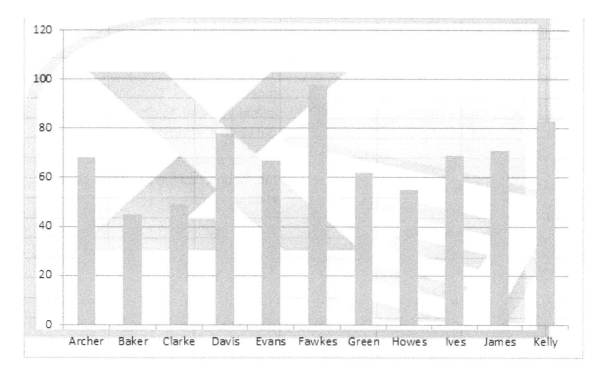

Chapter 3 Formatting your work

Page Formatting

The power of Excel is that it is a superb number crunching machine. On top of that it has lots of tools to help you present your information.

Whether you intend sharing a copy of your spreadsheet or providing a print out, you'll need to get to grips with page layout.

Essentially, this is controlling how your work will look. In this section you will see how you can add, delete hide and unhide pages in your workbook; How to change the page layout and how the page appears on screen and on paper and you will see how to use Office Themes.

By default, Excel has three worksheets created in every new workbook. You have already seen how to add and delete worksheets. You have seen how you can change your defaults to set Excel to create more or less worksheets when you create a new document.

There are times when you may wish to hide worksheets. One common reason is that you wish to display a summary, but keep the original data from view.

To hide a worksheet, right click on the tab, to bring up the list. Then click Hide.

Figure 176 Hide and Unhide a worksheet

You are not able to hide all the worksheets in the workbook.

Figure 177 You must keep one worksheet visible

To unhide a work sheet, right click on the tab of any unhidden worksheet, and you will be presented with the Unhide dialogue box.

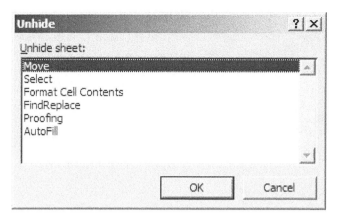

Figure 178 Unhide a worksheet

Select the sheet you want unhidden and click OK. You cannot unhide more than one sheet at a time.

The Page Layout tab has all the functions that you need to change how you work will look.

You will soon get to know what your preferred options are.

Setting the page margins is important when printing out your document. There are several pre-set layouts, plus the last custom layout used.

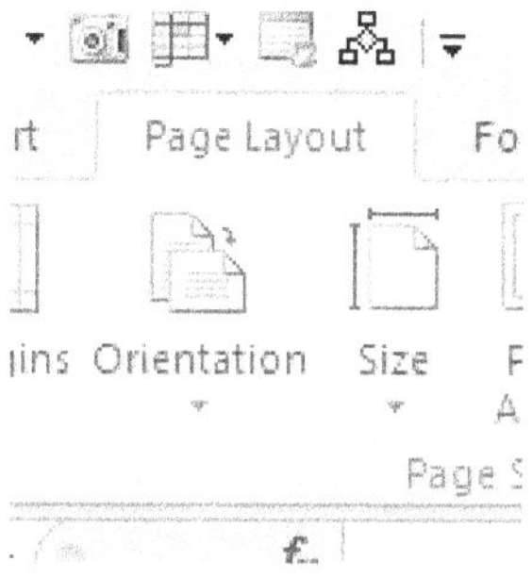

As well as the descriptions, the measurements of the pre-sets are given.

Clicking custom margin on the list opens the page set up dialogue box open on the page tab.

From here you can precisely customise your settings of how you want a page to appear.

The margins are the blank area surrounding your work, in the same way you have margins in a book. If you are going to file your document in a ring binder, you may want to increase the left margin for portrait layout, or the top margin for landscape layout.

Figure 179 Page Layout tab

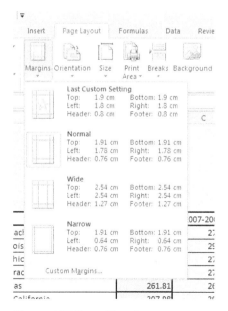

Figure 180 Page Margins

The header is an area at the top of the page. Typically you will include your title here. The footer is the area at the bottom of the page. Typically you will put page numbers here.

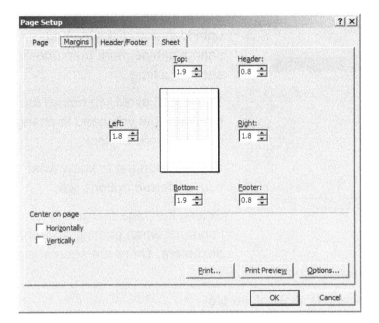

Figure 181 Custom page margins

However, it is your document; you can change the settings to your personal or corporate taste.

NOTE: This dialogue box can also be opened by clicking on the dialogue box launcher on the ribbon

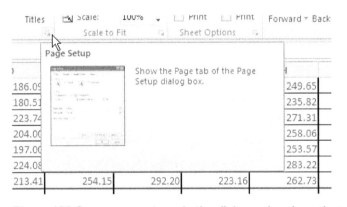

Figure 182 Open page set up via the dialogue box launcher

I often find it easier to set my page orientation out before I enter anything on the worksheet. However, you may not work that way or have other reasons to change the layout during your work.

These icons give you the choice of Portrait (long side vertical) or Landscape (long side horizontal).

Figure 183 Page orientation - Portrait or Landscape?

Size refers to the size of paper you will be printing out from. By clicking on More Paper Sizes you will bring up the page layout dialogue box.

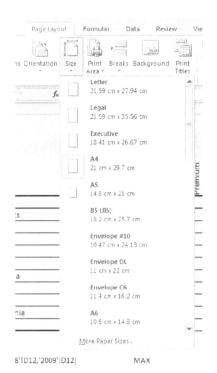

Figure 184 Paper size

You may find that you wish to print 2 sheets tall and one sheet wide, with the top row repeated on the second page. Use this dialogue box to do it from.

To select only a portion of your worksheet that you wish to print, you must highlight the cells, then Print Area. When you come to print out, it is only this area that will appear.

If at any time you find that you can't print all your worksheet, check this setting as you may have set a print area previously.

Depending on how much data you have on your worksheet, you may wish to split it into more than one printed page (insert a page break), have rows repeated at the top or columns repeated at the left.

If you click on the print titles icon, it will bring up the page set up dialogue box.

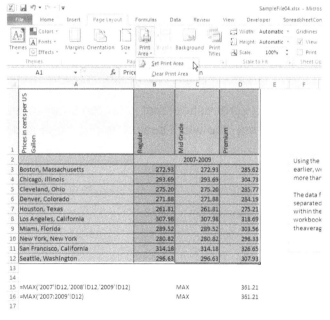

Figure 185 Select Print Area

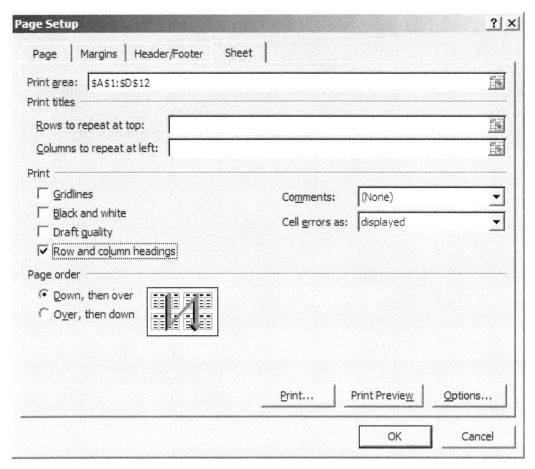

Figure 186 Sheet settings

You can also choose to have your work displayed over as many pages tall and wide as you need, or to have it scaled on to one sheet.

You often see a spreadsheet that is far too small to read comfortably. One way round this is to have, say, the width scaled as one page and the Height as two pages.

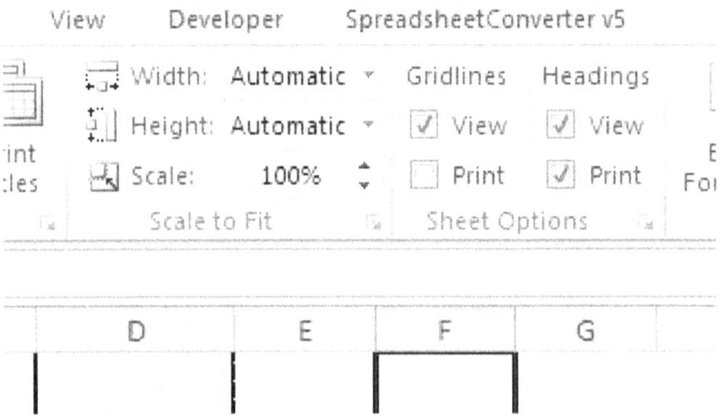

Figure 187 Page width and height

When I work, I like to see grid and any headings. I don't necessarily like these to print. You can choose your preferred options here.

You may include additional elements in your spreadsheet. For instance you might include graphs, images, notes and a logo. These can be found by clicking the Insert tab.

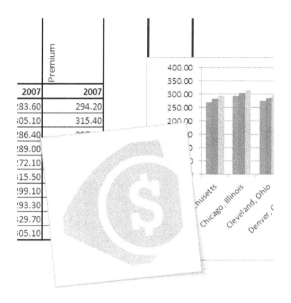

These elements can be ordered as to which you have at the front, or at the back. If you have more than 2 elements, you can send each further forward or back, depending upon your design.

In this instance the $ picture is at the front, positioned above a chart and the worksheet data.

Figure 188 Bring object to the front

In this case, it has been placed behind the graph

NOTE: in both cases they stay in front of the data on the worksheet.

You can choose to add headers and footers. You will best find your own personal style by playing around with the settings. You may have a corporate layout that you must adhere to.

I prefer to include the file name and the date and time it was printed.

Using the page set up dialogue box you can add logos, pictures and change the headers and footers to suit.

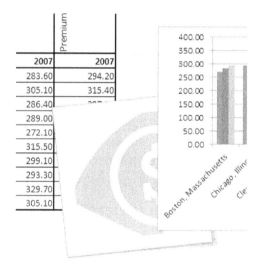

Figure 189 Move object to the back

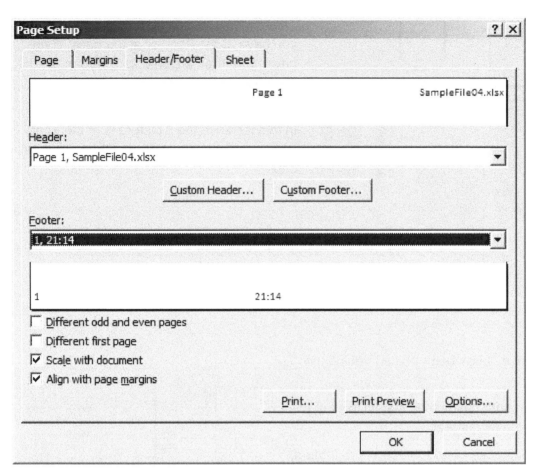

Figure 190 Headers and footers

By clicking Preview, you can see how your page will look when it is printed. You can continue to make changes at this stage.

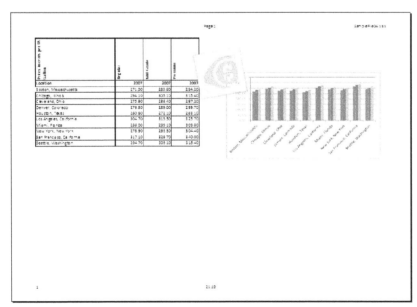

Figure 191 Print Preview

There are pre-set themes that you may use in deciding your page layout. These cover colours, fonts and effects. They are easy to apply. You can see the changes previewed as you alter the theme or the section of the theme.

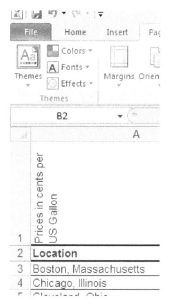

A word of caution: It is very easy to waste a lot of time playing with themes. Remember to concentrate on what message your information is to convey. The defaults are pretty good at presenting in a clear and concise manner.

Figure 192 Page Themes

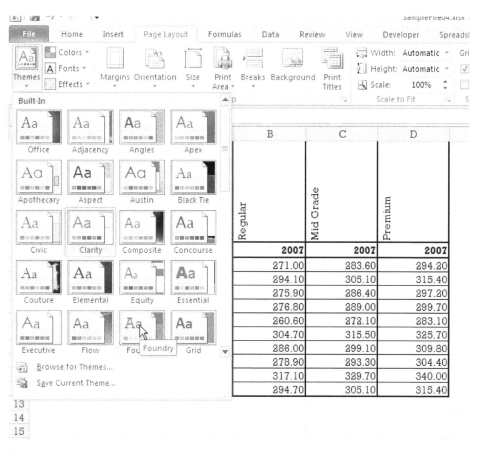

	B	C	D
Regular	Mid Grade	Premium	
2007	**2007**	**2007**	
271.00	283.60	294.20
294.10	305.10	315.40
275.90	286.40	297.20
276.80	289.00	299.70
260.60	272.10	283.10
304.70	315.50	325.70
286.00	299.10	309.80
278.90	293.30	304.40
317.10	329.70	340.00
294.70	305.10	315.40

Figure 193 Built in Themes

By all means play around and investigate, but don't let it replace real work that needs to be done!

On sheet formatting

You have seen how to look at the formatting the page itself. You are now going to see how you can make changes on the page. You will see how to format cells, change sizes of rows and columns, as well as adding rows and columns.

You can format cells using the Home tab, or you can right click on a cell. There are also keyboard commands that you can employ.

An easy way to demonstrate the changes you can make is to first select one cell, and then make one change. This will let you see the range of changes you can make. Then you will make changes to several cells, and make several changes at one time.

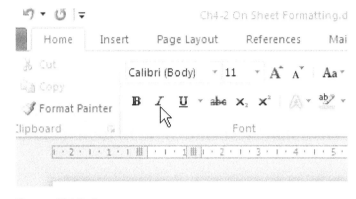

Figure 194 Italic

Select a cell on one of your worksheets with some text in it (rather than a number). In this example we will select the cell which says Miami Florida.

Using the home tab, click on the italicised "I". This will change the contents of the cell to change to italic.

There are two other ways of achieving the same result. The first is to use the keyboard shortcut Ctrl+ I 9this toggles between italic and not italic). I use keyboard shortcuts a lot. Three easy to remember are Ctrl+ B to bold; Ctrl+ I to italicise and Ctrl+ U to underline.

You can select the entire cell or just parts of the cell to change.

Another way is to right click within the cell. This will present you with two boxes to make changes from.

7	Houston, Texas	260.60
8	Los Angeles, California	304.70
9	*Miami, Florida*	286.00
10	New York, New York	278.90
11	San Francisco, California	317.10
12	Seattle, Washington	294.70
13	Average per year	285.98
14		

Figure 195 Italicised text

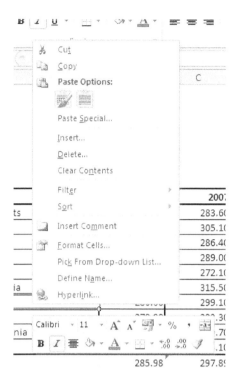

Figure 196 Right click within the cell and select Format Cells

The most relevant is the mini format tool bar at the bottom. The most common format changes are located here.

You could also click on Format Cells in the large toolbar.

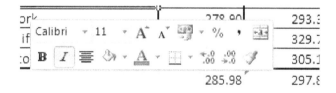

Figure 197 Mini Format Toolbar

The icons on the mini tool bar are fairly self-explanatory. You may wish to experiment with each icon in turn, but for now click the B to embolden the cell contents.

There are many changes that you can make. To see them all select a cell and click on any of the Dialogue Box Launchers on the Home tab.

Alternatively, use the keyboard shortcut Ctrl+ Shift+ F

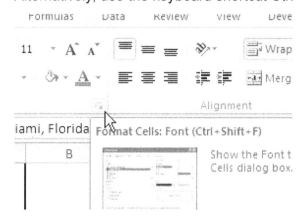

Figure 198 Format Dialogue Box Launcher

It is from this single dialogue box that you can make one or many changes. You can change the font, alignment, cell border and fill.

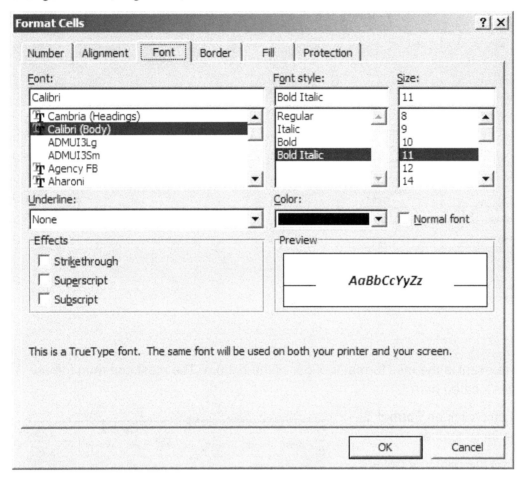

Figure 199 Format Cells Dialogue Box

In practice, you would usually only change one or two options. If you change too many, your spreadsheet can become difficult to read and may confuse your viewer.

Using the different tabs, experiment by changing the font type size and colour.

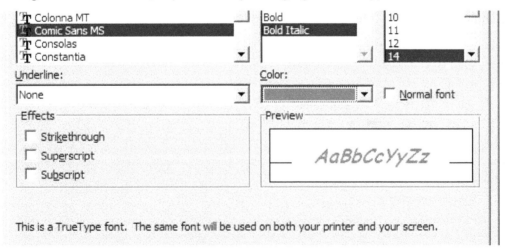

Figure 200 Change Font Type and Colour

Then change the border type and colour.

Finally change the cell Fill.

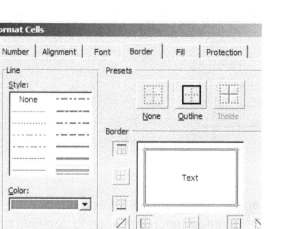

Figure 201 Change Border Type and Colour

There are several subordinate dialogue boxes which will enable you to have more choices.

It is time well spent experimenting to see what is available.

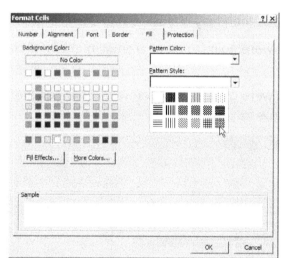

Figure 202 Change Cell Fill Colour

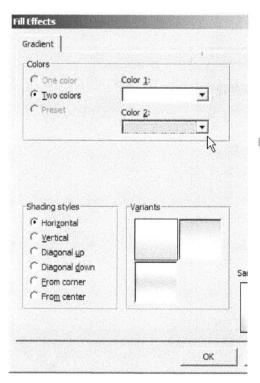

Figure 203 Fill - Subordinate Gradient Dialogue Box

This gives you a very wide range of choices that you can make to alter any cell in your workbook.

8	Los Angeles, California	304.
9	*Miami, Florida*	286.
10	New York, New York	278.
11	San Francisco, California	317.
12	Seattle, Washington	294.
13	Average per year	285.

Figure 204 Changes made to one cell

A word of caution – please use options sparingly. Too much colour and a fancy font with an interesting background could detract from the information you wish to convey. Just because you can, doesn't mean you should. If there's a valid reason to change, then go ahead, but try to make things easy on the eye.

To make changes to more than one cell, simply highlight them and then make the changes using your preferred method. For instance if you were going to just change to italicised then may choose just to use CTRL+ I.

If you were going to make a small number of changes you could use the mini format tool bar.

If you were going to make several changes then you would probably use the format dialogue box.

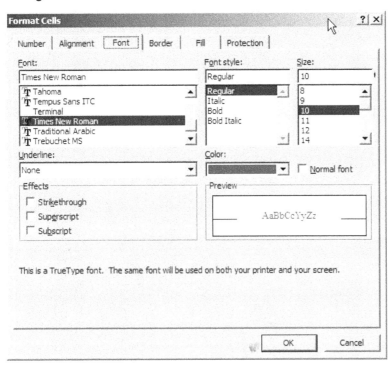

Figure 205 Making changes to multiple cells

You may also want to change the way your text changes, so you would use either the option from the ribbon or use the format cells dialogue box.

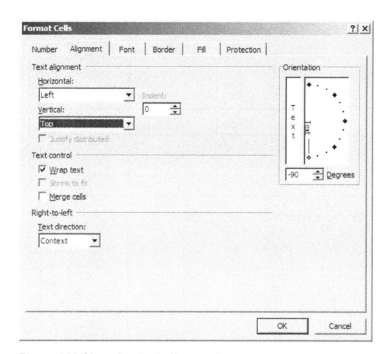

You can change the number format using the dialogue box or the ribbon. In this instance, the format is being changed to Accounting.

Figure 206 Changing text alignment

You could do this for individual cells or a number of cells.

It is good to experiment, but don't go too far!

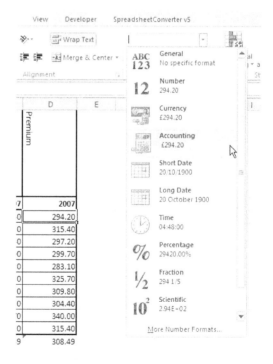

Figure 207 Changing number format

G21	f_x			
	A	B	C	D
1	Prices in cents per US Gallon	Regular	Mid Grade	Premium
2	Location	2007	2007	2007
3	Boston, Massachusetts	271.00	283.60	294.20
4	Chicago, Illinois	294.10	305.10	315.40
5	Cleveland, Ohio	275.90	286.40	297.20
6	Denver, Colorado	276.80	289.00	299.70
7	Houston, Texas	260.60	272.10	283.10
8	Los Angeles, California	304.70	315.50	325.70
9	Miami, Florida	286.00	299.10	309.80
10	New York, New York	278.90	293.30	304.40
11	San Francisco, California	317.10	329.70	340.00
12	Seattle, Washington	294.70	305.10	315.40
13	Average per year	£285.98	£297.89	£308.49
14				
15				

Figure 208 Too much formatting can hurt your eyes!

Change row Heights and Column widths

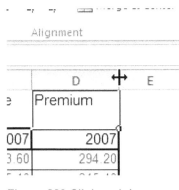

Figure 209 Click and drag column width

There are several ways to change the column width and row heights. The first option is to bring your mouse over the row or column header border, until the mouse icon changes to a double headed arrow.

Then simply click and drag to the desired height or width.

If you require more precise control, then select the column or row (s) you wish to change. Then right click and select column width or row height.

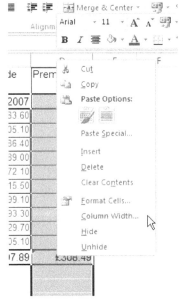

Figure 210 Change height or width - Precise Control

You then enter the particular height or width that you want.

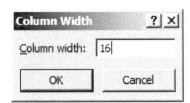

Figure 211 Column width

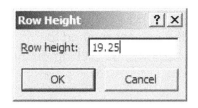

Figure 212 Row height

Most people will stick with the default sizes all the time. But increasing one row or column can add emphasis. It is a particularly good way to show a results column/row.

The measurement used is a POINT. There are 72 points in an inch. You don't need to remember this, as the best way to decide what the best size is to experiment. There is no "correct" size.

You can set the option to show the mini tool bar, or otherwise, on the File tab, Options, General. This is set to be on by default.

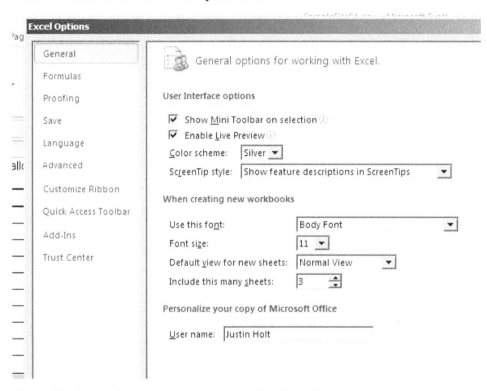

Figure 213 General option to show mini tool bar by default

AutoFit

Auto Fit is a very useful feature of Excel. To change the width or height of your cell to match the contents, select the edge of column or row you wish to change (it works for both). Your cursor will turn in to a double headed arrow. Double click and the column or row will change size.

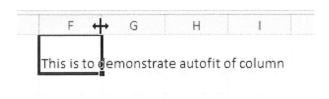

Figure 214 AutoFit Column

3	Bostor
4	Chicac
5	Clevel:
6	Denvei
7	Houst(

The result is that the column or row adjusts to fit.

I find double click on the row or column grid the easiest method to remember and use. The same result can be achieved by clicking on the Format icon on the Home tab.

Figure 215
AutoFit Row

This is to demonstrate autofit of column

Figure 216 AutoFitted column

Figure 217 AutoFit list

Insert Row or Column

To insert a row, highlight the row you wish to be below the inserted row. Then on the home tab, Cells click Insert.

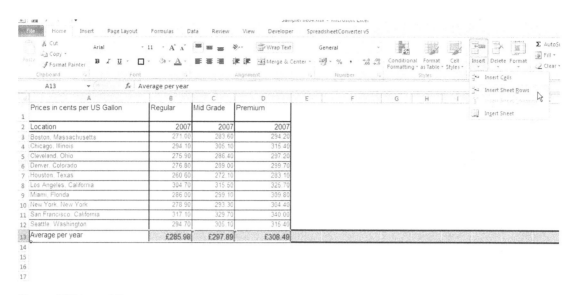

Figure 218 Insert Row

You will be presented with a list. Select Insert Sheet Rows.

You can see the result of the added row below (MAX formula has been used).

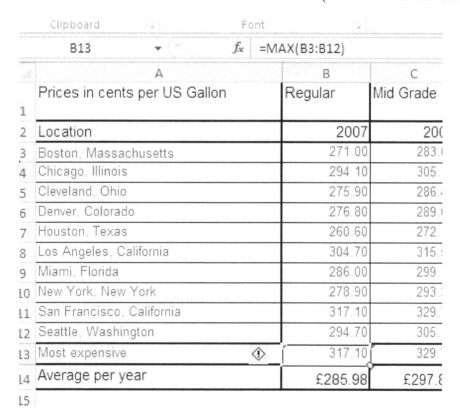

	A	B	C
	Prices in cents per US Gallon	Regular	Mid Grade
1			
2	Location	2007	200
3	Boston, Massachusetts	271.00	283.
4	Chicago, Illinois	294.10	305.
5	Cleveland, Ohio	275.90	286.
6	Denver, Colorado	276.80	289.
7	Houston, Texas	260.60	272.
8	Los Angeles, California	304.70	315.
9	Miami, Florida	286.00	299.
10	New York, New York	278.90	293.
11	San Francisco, California	317.10	329.
12	Seattle, Washington	294.70	305.
13	Most expensive	317.10	329.
14	Average per year	£285.98	£297.8
15			

B13 — f_x =MAX(B3:B12)

Figure 219 "Most expensive" row has been added [=MAX (B3:B12)]

Inserting a column is very similar. Highlight the column that is to the right of where you want the column to be added. You can, as before click Insert, but this time choose Insert Sheet Columns. You may wish to highlight the column and right click and choose Insert.

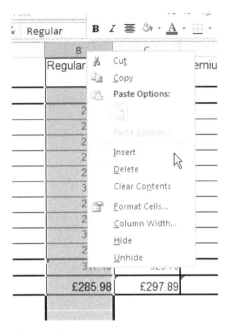

Note you may wish to change the size of the column afterwards.

In this instance we have added a column to calculate from the text in column A, the state.

Figure 220 Insert column

| | B3 | ▼ | fx | =RIGHT(A3,LEN(A3)-FIND(" ",A3)) |

	A	B	C
1	Prices in cents per US Gallon	State	Regular
2	Location		2(
3	Boston, Massachusetts	Massachusetts	271
4	Chicago, Illinois	Illinois	294
5	Cleveland, Ohio	Ohio	275
6	Denver, Colorado	Colorado	276
7	Houston, Texas	Texas	260
8	Los Angeles, California	California	304
9	Miami, Florida	Florida	286
10	New York, New York	New York	278
11	San Francisco, California	California	317
12	Seattle, Washington	Washington	294
13	Most expensive		317
14	Average per year		£285
15			

Figure 221 Column added

Format Painter

Figure 222 Format painter on Home tab

Prices in cents per US Gallon	State	Regular	Mid Grade
Location		2007	2007
Boston, Massachusetts	Massachusetts	271.00	283.60
Chicago, Illinois	Illinois	294.10	305.10
Cleveland, Ohio	Ohio	275.90	286.40
Denver, Colorado	Colorado	276.80	289.00
Houston, Texas	Texas	260.60	272.10
Los Angeles, California	California	304.70	315.50
Miami, Florida	Florida	286.00	299.10
New York, New York	New York	278.90	293.30
San Francisco, California	California	317.10	329.70
Seattle, Washington	Washington	294.70	305.10
Most expensive		317.10	329.70
Average per year		285.98	297.89

You may have set a format in some cells (single cell or multiple cells) that you wish to use elsewhere.

In this case we have chosen to have column C to be left aligned. To share this format with other cells, you highlight them, and then click Format Painter on the home tab.

Select the cell or cells you wish to receive the format and then release your mouse. In this case the cells in column D and E will then left align.

	C	D	E
	Regular	Mid Grade	Premium
	2007	2007	2007
etts	271.00	283.60	294.20
	294.10	305.10	315.40
	275.90	286.40	297.20
	276.80	289.00	299.70
	260.60	272.10	283.10
	304.70	315.50	325.70
	286.00	299.10	309.80
	278.90	293.30	304.40
	317.10	329.70	340.00
	294.70	305.10	315.40
	317.10	329.70	340.00
	285.98	297.89	308.49

Figure 223 Format painter in action

Delete Row or Column

The process to delete a column or row is the opposite of inserting. Highlight the row or column you wish to delete. Then select Delete and chose Delete Sheet Rows/Columns. This works for multiple rows or columns.

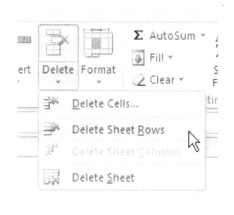

Figure 224 Delete sheet row

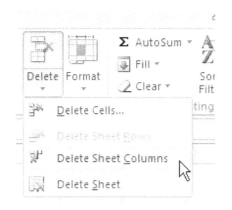

Figure 225 Delete sheet column

If you make a mistake, remember to use the keyboard shortcut Ctrl+ Z.

You can also highlight the row or column, right click and choose delete.

Conditional formatting

Conditional Formatting allows you to set rules which will format cells depending on their value.

In this instance, we want the above average cost cells to be highlighted in red and bold.

Click on the Conditional Formatting icon and select New Rule. The New Formatting Rule dialogue box appears.

There are many options, and we are choosing to highlight the cells that are above average cost.

Figure 226 Conditional formatting - New Rule

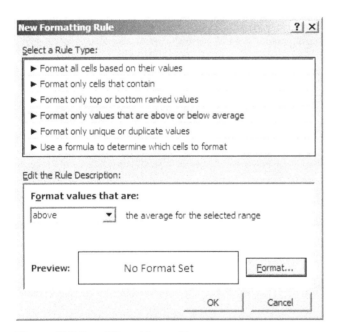

Figure 227 Conditional formatting –
New Formatting Rule

Chose Format Only Values that are above or below average.

Click on Format and choose the settings that you prefer.

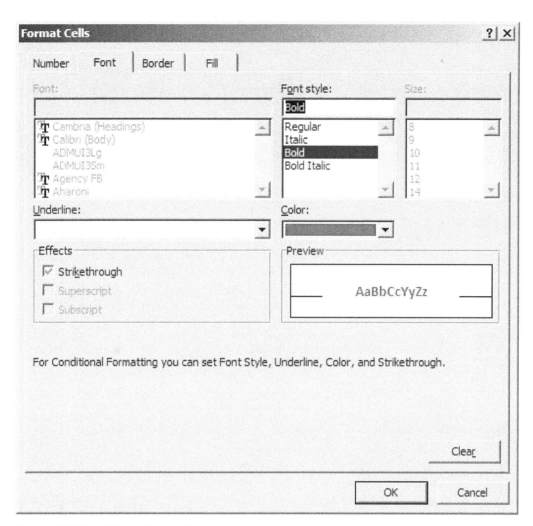

Figure 228 Conditional formatting - dialogue box to choose options

Then Click OK and OK.

You can select all the cells at one go, or you can choose to use Format Painter.

B	C	D	E
State	Regular	Mid Grade	Premium
	2007	2007	2007
Massachusetts	271.00	283.60	294.20
Illinois	**294.10**	**305.10**	**315.40**
Ohio	275.90	286.40	297.20
Colorado	276.80	289.00	299.70
Texas	260.60	272.10	283.10
California	**304.70**	**315.50**	**325.70**
Florida	**286.00**	299.10	**309.80**
New York	278.90	293.30	304.40

Figure 229 conditionally formatted cells

Hiding Rows or Columns

It may be appropriate to hide rows or columns of data, usually to emphasise your results. The method works for both rows and columns. This is illustrated here only using rows.

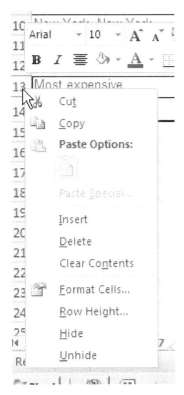

Figure 230 Hide row

Highlight the Row or Column you wish to hide by clicking on the Row or column label (e.g. A or 13). Click Hide.

You can see in the figure below that in this instance Row 13 is hidden.

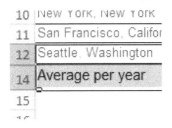

Figure 231 Hidden row

This can be useful to hide formulas or look ups from casual users of your spreadsheets. NOTE: if you have any formulas in hidden cells, they still are there and still return results.

To unhide rows or columns highlight the adjacent rows or columns and right click. Select Unhide.

If you have multiple hidden rows and columns, you can simply click at the top left of your worksheet (between the A and 1) which highlights the whole worksheet.

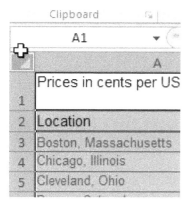

Figure 232 Select the entire worksheet

Then right click and unhide.

Format as a Table

Help improve the look and feel of your worksheet by formatting your cells within your worksheet as a TABLE.

You can analyse records using Table. It has some database qualities, which will be looked at in another section.

Select the cells concerned then click Format as Table.

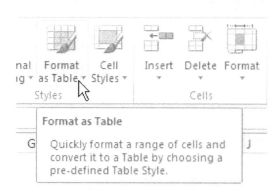

Figure 233 format as a table

You will see a grid of table formats to choose from.

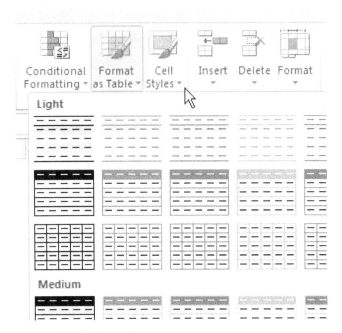

Figure 234 Table options

At this stage, simply experiment to see which layout suits your data.

You will be presented with the Format As Table dialogue box.

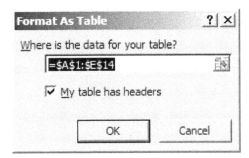

Figure 235 Format as table dialogue box

As the area was preselected, the values are already included. The formula "=$A$1:$E$14" refers to the area highlighted. The $ is an absolute reference. You encountered absolute references and relative cell references previously.

The figure below shows a formatted table. The down arrows next to the header text allow you to filter the records produced.

Prices in cents per US Gallon	State	Regular	Mid Grade	Premium
Location		2007	2007	2007
Boston, Massachusetts	Massachusetts	271.00	283.60	294.20
Chicago, Illinois	Illinois	294.10	305.10	315.40
Cleveland, Ohio	Ohio	275.90	286.40	297.20
Denver, Colorado	Colorado	276.80	289.00	299.70
Houston, Texas	Texas	260.60	272.10	283.10
Los Angeles, California	California	304.70	315.50	325.70
Miami, Florida	Florida	286.00	299.10	309.80
New York, New York	New York	278.90	293.30	304.40
San Francisco, California	California	317.10	329.70	340.00
Seattle, Washington	Washington	294.70	305.10	315.40
Most expensive		317.10	329.70	340.00
Average per year		285.98	297.89	308.49

Figure 236 A range of cells formatted as a table

For now, do not worry about these as they will be looked at in another context.

Chapter 4 Charts

- Resizing charts
- Moving charts
- Change chart type
- Editing Chart Elements
- Manipulating your charts
- Adding data labels to your chart
- Different chart types
- Column Chart
- Line Chart
- Pie Chart
- Bar Chart
- Dynamic Charts, Sparklines and In-Cell Charts

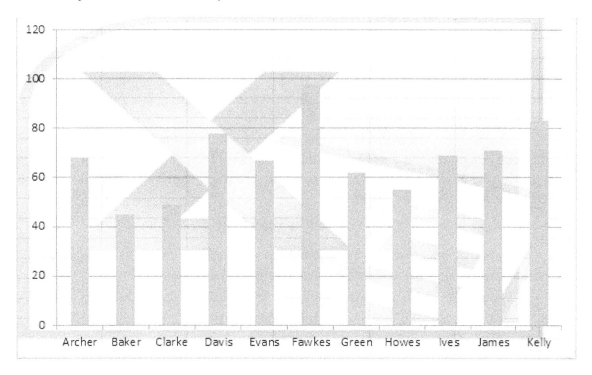

Chapter 4 Charts

In this section you will see how to create a very simple chart from data in your worksheet and will be introduced to the names of the component parts of the chart.

You may wish to create a worksheet to follow along with. The contents of the cells are unimportant, as long as you have students, subjects and results.

Cell Reference	Contents	Format
A1:A12	Surname	Text
A1:I1	Exam Subject	Text
B2:I12	Exam Result	Number, no decimal places

	Maths	English Lit.	English Lang.	History	Geography	French	Biology	Chemistry
Archer	68	87	83	76	84	86	88	90
Baker	45	83	79	72	89	97	104	112
Clarke	49	88	83	82	99	108	118	127
Davis	78	79	71	74	71	69	67	65
Evans	67	55	64	63	62	61	61	61
Fawke	98	93	80	82	73	67	61	55
Green	62	68	67	70	73	75	77	79
Holt	55	87	76	74	85	89	94	98
Ives	69	74	74	72	75	75	76	77
James	71	73	81	83	88	92	97	101
Kelly	83	85	81	79	78	76	75	73

Figure 237 Charting exam results

The purpose of a chart is to present your data in an easy to understand format. The examples here are from small selections of data. In reality, you may be creating charts based upon data many times larger.

There is a simple "plan" to follow in creating a good chart

- Know what message you are trying to convey – this will help you chose the type of graph to use and how to show your message to its best advantage
- Sort your data – this helps in presenting your chart clearly and effectively
- Prepare your chart – often using the predefined charts

Format the chart to its best advantage – this doesn't mean fill it full of graphics. Often "less is more".

This example will use a TABLE of exam results for a number of students. Once you have sorted the data, in this case by student name, SELECT the data to be charted. This can be done by clicking and dragging. The data is said to be selected CONTIGUOUSLY when adjoining rows and columns are selected. If only some rows or some columns were selected, and these were not adjacent to each other, they would be described as NON-CONTIGUOUSLY selected.

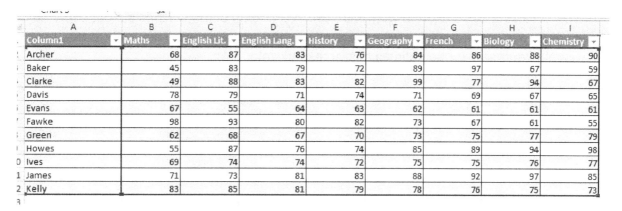

Column1	Maths	English Lit.	English Lang.	History	Geography	French	Biology	Chemistry
Archer	68	87	83	76	84	86	88	90
Baker	45	83	79	72	89	97	67	59
Clarke	49	88	83	82	99	77	94	67
Davis	78	79	71	74	71	69	67	65
Evans	67	55	64	63	62	61	61	61
Fawke	98	93	80	82	73	67	61	55
Green	62	68	67	70	73	75	77	79
Howes	55	87	76	74	85	89	94	98
Ives	69	74	74	72	75	75	76	77
James	71	73	81	83	88	92	97	85
Kelly	83	85	81	79	78	76	75	73

Figure 238 Raw data converted to a table

After selecting the data click on the Inset tab, and chose the type of graph you want to create from the Charts Group. Select Column.

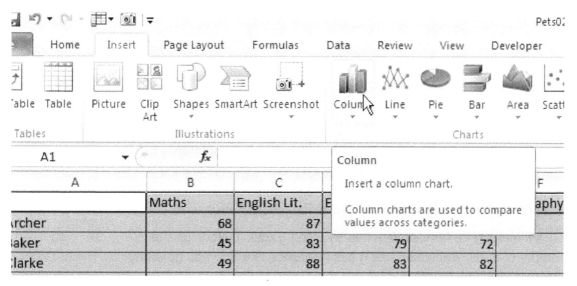

Figure 239 Insert Column Chart

On clicking Column you will see a Gallery of many options for column graphs. To keep it simple, select the 2-D clustered column – this is the first option.

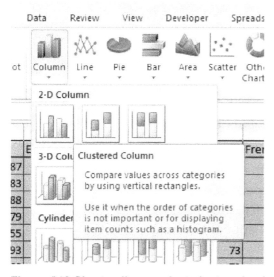

Figure 240 Chart gallery - select clustered column

This creates a basic chart to work with. We see graphs of many kinds almost every day, whether it is in text books, newspapers or in news programmes. They are created to visually represent (or sometimes misrepresent) data.

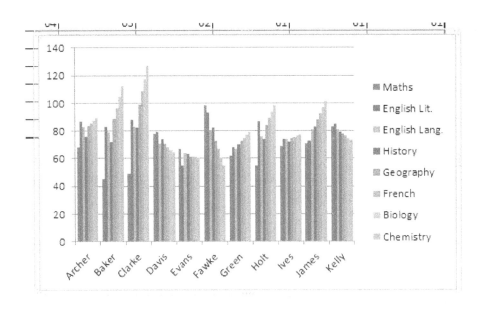

Figure 241 2D clustered column chart

A 2-D (two dimensional) graph has two AXIS. The horizontal axis is called the X axis. The vertical axis is called the Y axis. Where the X and Y axis meet is called the origin. (To read up on this use your favourite search engine to look up "Cartesian coordinate system".

You will already be familiar with this by using Excel. To look up the contents of a cell you would use a cell reference like E6. You go along the x axis until you locate E, and use the Y axis to find 6.

Figure 242 Chart legend

What a graph will do is PLOT the location of the DATA POINTS. Your Excel graph will place a DATA MARKER at this data point.

Often you will want to display some form of LEGEND in your chart. In this instance it is positioned to the Right of the chart. You will see how it can be positioned elsewhere shortly.

There are other elements of the chart to note.

The groups of different coloured bars are known as a DATA SERIES. In this example, a colour represents a different subject. On the chart, there is a BACK GROUND which can be edited if it enhances your message.

Figure 243 Chart legend

There are GRIDLINES which help to put context to the figures displayed. The gridlines in this chart are set to appear at every change in 20 marks. These are known as MAJOR GRIDLINES. These are customisable, and could equally have been set to appear to change every 10 or 25 marks.

MINOR GRIDLINES could be added to the chart if they add clarity or perspective. For example, as the major gridlines are set to every 20, minor gridlines could be set at say 5 or 10 marks.

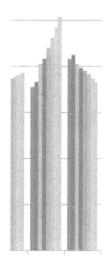

Figure 244 Chart elements
- data series, gridlines and data series

Note that in each change in data series there is a TICK MARK.

Every ELEMENT in the chart can be edited. This can be done to emphasise your data. The "rule" to follow is to ask if the changes make your message clearer to your audience or not? If it does, then do it.

Resizing charts

Perhaps the simplest form of editing you can do to your chart is to re-size it or to move it. To help with this there are 8 HANDLES on your chart. There is one in each corner and one at the midpoint of each side. I like to think of these mid points as being North, South, East and West.

By positioning the cursor on one of these handles, then clicking and dragging, the chart area will increase or decrease as you drag.

It is worthwhile experimenting with this. In general though, just clicking and dragging will distort your chart. For example you could easily make the columns appear far too big by clicking and dragging on the "South" handle.

Figure 245 Chart elements
- data series, gridlines and data series

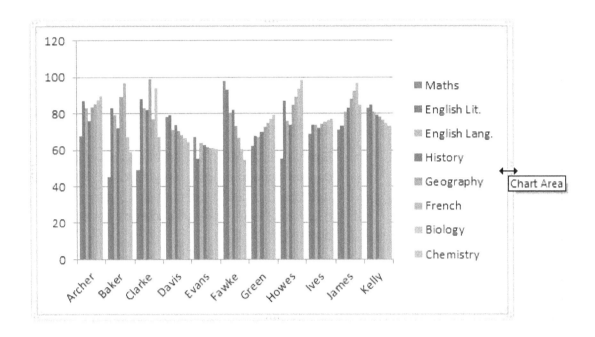

Figure 246 Resizing charts

To avoid this distortion, hold the shift key down as you select and then drag. This keeps the elements in the same ratio as before.

Placing your cursor over the chart area will make it change to the standard Windows move cursor. Click and drag to the location you want your graph to appear.

Moving charts

Placing your cursor over the chart area will make it change to the standard Windows move cursor. Click and drag to the location you want your graph to appear.

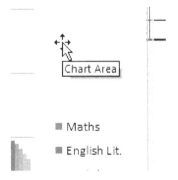

Figure 247 Move chart cursor

You can move your chart to a new worksheet. There are several ways that you may wish to do this. You can simply highlight your chart, CUT or COPY and then PASTE in to another worksheet. I tend to use this most of all, and I use the keyboard short cuts of Ctrl-C (or Ctrl-X) then Ctrl-V when at the new location. I find this to be the quickest method for me.

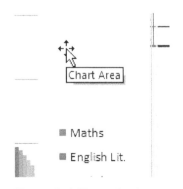

Figure 248 Move chart cursor

However, as an alternative, right click anywhere in the chart and you will see a menu appear. Click MOVE CHART

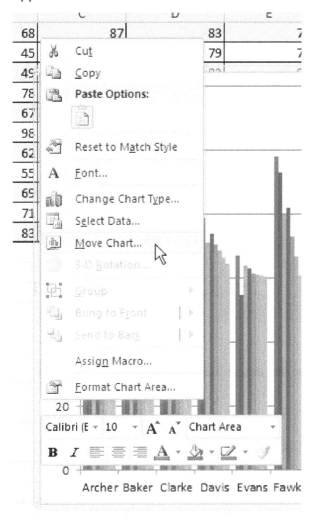

Figure 249 Move chart menu

Using the dialogue box chose the location your chart is to be moved to. In the figure below the RADIO BUTTON for New Sheet has been selected. You can rename the default Chart1 to any other meaningful name.

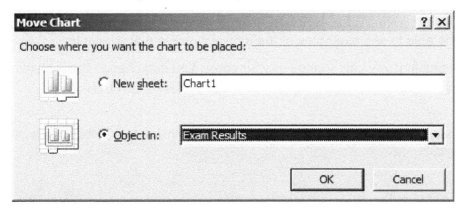

Figure 250 Move chart dialogue box

This will place the chart in a new worksheet.

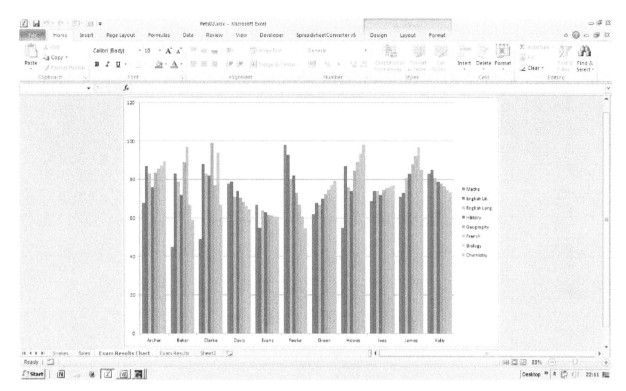

Figure 251 Chart in a new worksheet

You can create your chart using the icons on the Insert Tab. However, you may wish to click on the Chart Dialogue Box Launcher.

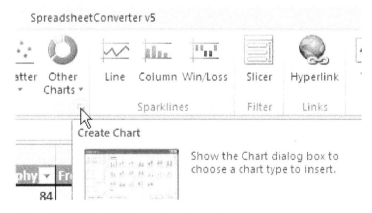

Figure 252 Chart dialogue box launcher

From here you will be able to see examples of the different charts that available.

There are many options that you can change in your chart. You can change the look of the entire chart using defaults. You can change individual CHART ELEMENTS after selecting them.

I find it is easier to select the elements when I have increased the zoom. I often use a zoom of around 150%.

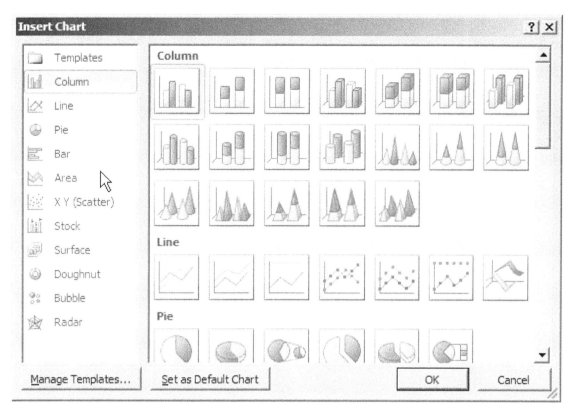

Figure 253 Insert chart gallery

If your graph does not display the information in your data clearly enough, or you want to experiment a little, you can change the chart type.

Change chart type

If you have been following along with this example you created a 2D bar chart. To change this, select the entire chart, and then right click. There is a menu option called Change Chart Type. Click this. Choose the 4th icon from the left. This is the 3D Clustered Column. Select this then click OK.

Figure 254 Change chart type

This is sufficiently different for you to see that the chart has changed, but not so different that the meaning is lost.

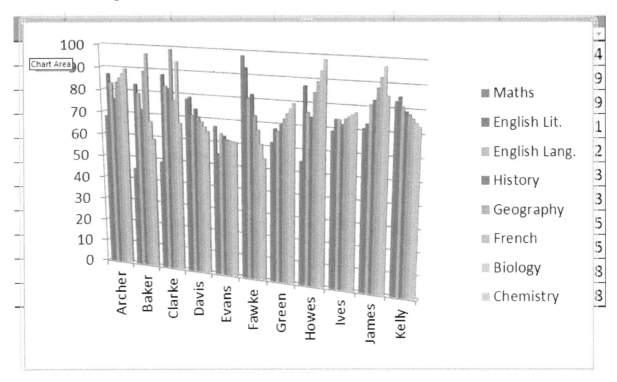

Figure 255 3D clustered column chart

There are hundreds of options available. Going through every one is unnecessary. Once you have seen how to change an entire chart, you can see how to change to any type. All you need to do is experiment a little.

It will be the same with chart elements, once you have seen how to change one element; you will know how to change all of the others.

When you select the chart, you will notice that there are additional tabs. These are CONTEXTUAL TABS.

Click on the contextual chart tools tab. In this instance the chart is style 2. Change this to style 26.

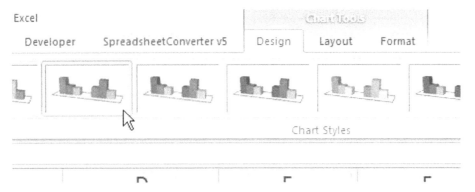

Figure 256 Contextual charts tabs – Design

The differences can be quite subtle, as they are in this case. Had you changed the style to say, Style 1 the differences may be dramatic. In this case it would likely make your information more difficult to see.

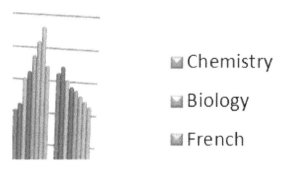

Figure 257 Note changes to the chart

It is also possible to change the layout of the chart in one go. When you look at the Chart Layout group, you will see that Layout 10 has been chosen. This is very simple.

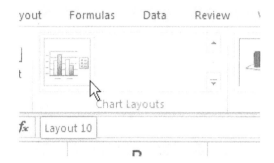

Figure 258 Chart Layouts

Select Layout 9 and the chart becomes more informative with editable titles for the chart and for the axis. To edit the titles, click on them and overtype.

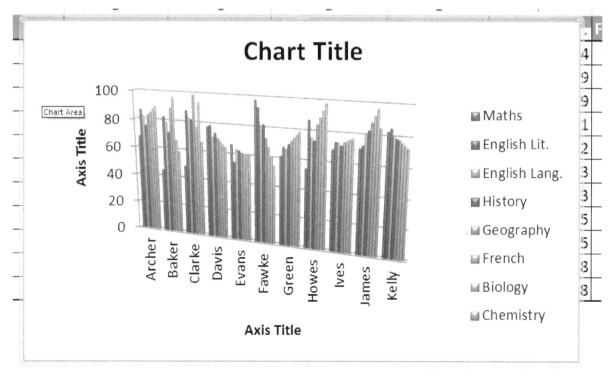

Figure 259 Select chart titles

In this exercise, replace Chart Title with Exam Results.

To demonstrate some of the ways you can manipulate your chart, here is a simplified version of the previous chart. Here, only the maths results were selected before the chart was created.

To edit any particular chart element simply select then right click that element.

In this case, the legend makes no sense, so delete it. Change the colour of the series or an individual. So we can change the colour to green by selecting them all.

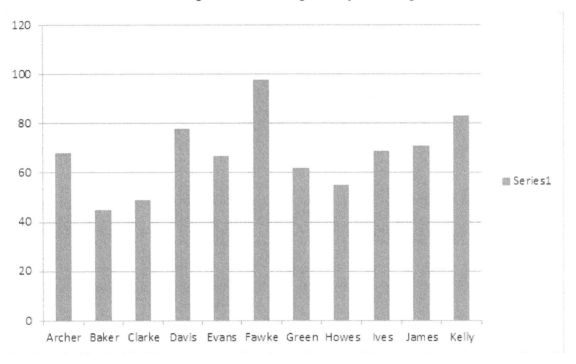

Figure 260 Chart based on one exam result

There are always several ways to achieve a particular result. In this case by selecting then right clicking the series, we can select the fill (paint pot icon) and change this to green. We could have equally well achieved the same result by changing the design in the chart tools tab.

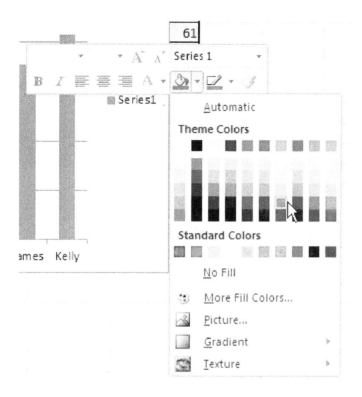

Figure 261 Change colours

By single clicking the series, all are highlighted and are showing their handles. You can click once more on a single person, and only that result is highlighted.

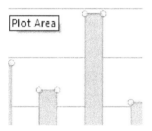

Figure 262 Select a single bar

There are many ways you can manipulate the a data point. One way would be to select a gradient fill. You may choose to put a pattern in, use a picture or any of the options in the dialogue box.

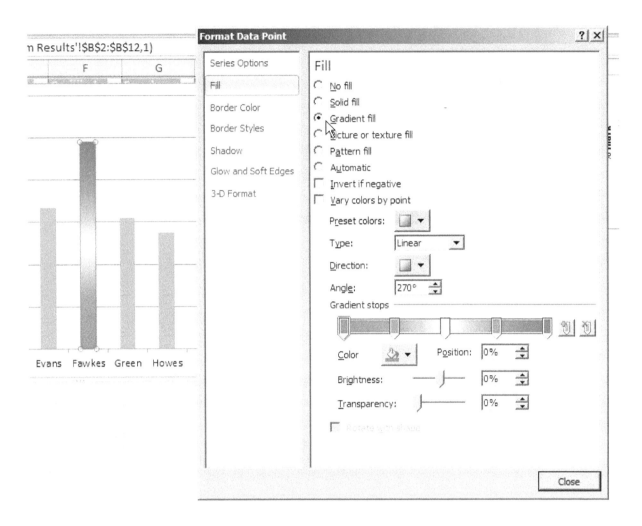

Figure 263 Edit a single data point

The key is to decide if the changes you make enhance your data or not. Just because you can change something, doesn't mean you should. The deciding factor is to ask if it adds clarity or aids understanding.

You will see from the dialogue box, that you can add borders, shadows or even a glow.

The best advice is to keep it simple if you are sharing your data. However, while you are learning how to use a feature, by all means experiment.

The example shown in the figure below may be an exaggeration, but it does indicate just how much you could manipulate each, or all elements.

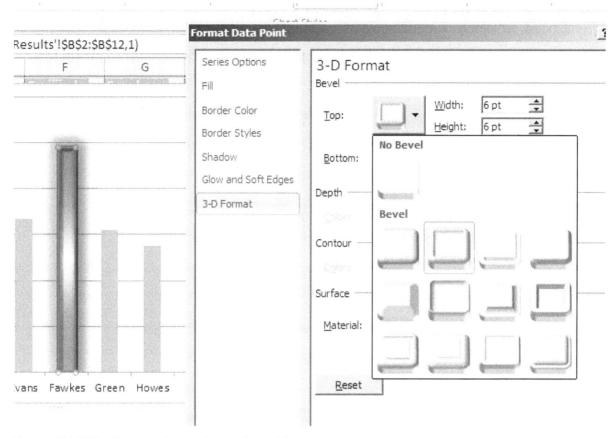

Figure 264 Edit a data point taken beyond good taste

You can always right click and then REVERT TO MATCH STYLE to bring some normality back to your chart.

You can format the plot area in a similar manner. Here, some clip art relating to maths has been inserted.

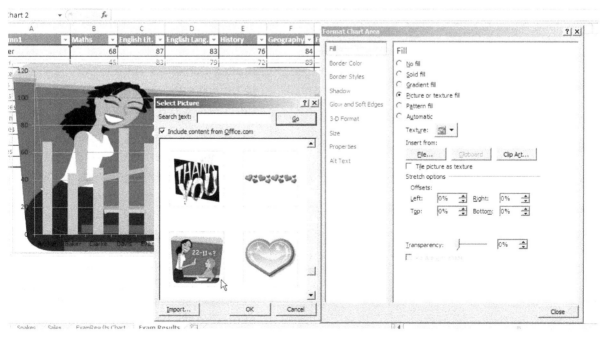

Figure 265 Adding graphics to the plot area

This may be a trivial example, but a company logo or other relevant image could be included. Or simply corporate colours could be used.

Again, less is usually more. To find out if a particular option helps simply try them to see.

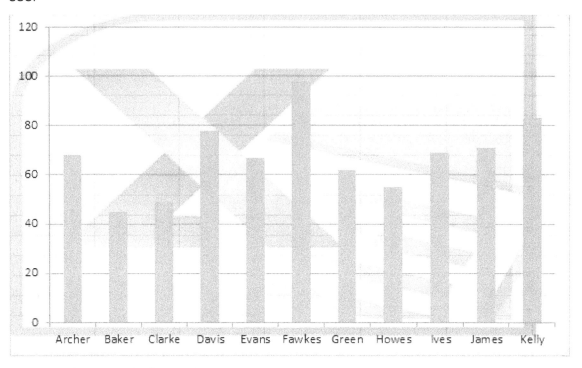

Manipulating your charts

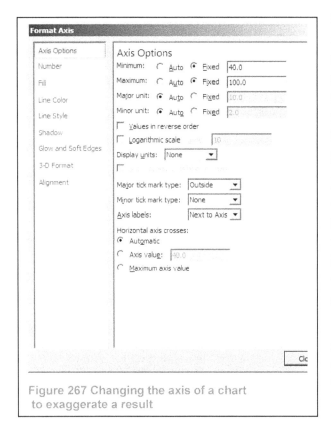

One way to manipulate a chart is to change how much of the axis is displayed. In this instance, the maximum percentage has been reduced from 120% to just 100%. This makes sense as there is very unlikely to be a greater score than 100%, particularly in a maths exam!

However, by making the minimum 40%, the difference in the grades appears to be exaggerated. In the example used here, the difference between Baker and Fawkes is large in any event. Baker had a result of 45% and Fawkes of 98%.

In the "natural order of things" it would make sense that the bar for Fawkes should really be just over double the height of that of Baker.

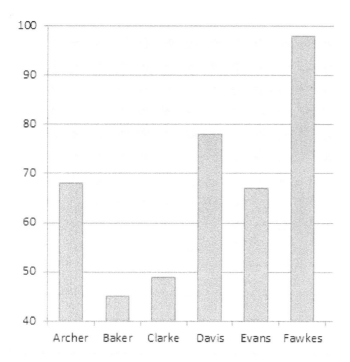

Figure 268 Manipulating the axis can distort the apparent relationship

This sort of manipulation is quite common. Often there are many innocent reasons for displaying data this way. However, one should be careful when reading a chart in, say, a newspaper or magazine, as they may be trying to add weight to an argument.

It is generally considered good practice, to have the axis start at zero, as this will show the relationship.

Adding a trend line can give a very good indication of how things are playing out in your data. To add a trend line, select the data series; then right click and choose add trend line.

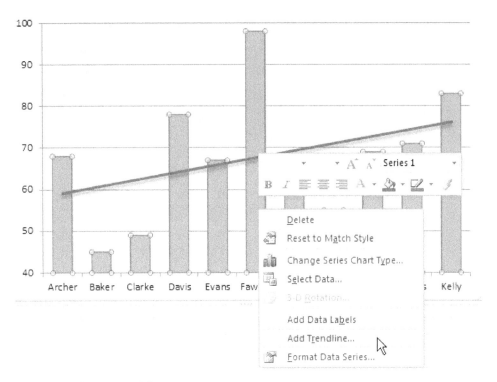

Figure 269 Add a trend line

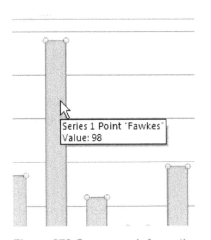

Figure 270 On-screen information within a chart

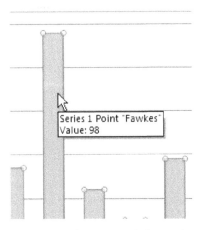

Figure 271 On-screen information within a chart

Caution is needed though. In this example, a trend is meaningless. Unless that is you do actually want to show how maths exam marks tend to increase in order of ascending alphabetical order of student surname!

It would make more sense to, say, plot a particular student's performance over a period, or perhaps the cumulative result of a class over a period. The key is to think about what you want to show, rather than what Excel can do.

Adding data labels to your chart

On screen your chart can display a great deal of information. For example, you can hover the mouse over and you will see an information box appear showing that students score.

When printing, it may be informative to add these. Right click on the data series and then ADD DATA LABLES.

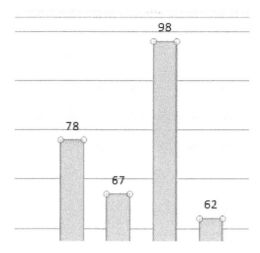

Figure 272 Data labels above

Like any other chart element, it is possible to edit the data labels. Select all or just one, and you will be able to right click and change the location, colour and alignment.

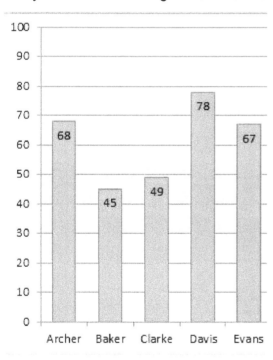

Figure 273 Data labels inside columns

Different chart types

You are able to display your data in many different chart styles. Once you have learnt how to edit your data in one type you will know the techniques you can use in all the others.

You should aim to keep your charts clear and only add what is important to support your message. There are different charts types that help with this.

In general:-

Column	Show variation over time
Line	Trends over time
Pie	For ONE data series - parts of the whole
Bar	Comparison over fixed period of time
Area	Relative values over time
X-Y	Show correlation
Stock	Show a high and low value
Donut	Like pie chart but for more than one data series
Surface	3D chart connecting a set of data points
Bubble analysis	Location and size can show relationships - often used in social and medical
Radar	Aggregate values of multiple variables; the length of each spoke changes for each variable
Sparkline's	Shows Trends
Others	Such as In Cell charts, pictogram and Gantt chart

	A	B
1	Chart Type	Appropriate use
2	Column	Show variation over time
3	Line	Trends over time
4	Pie	For ONE data series - parts of the whole
5	Bar	Comparison over fixed period of time
6	Area	Relative values over time
7	X-Y	Show correlation
8	Stock	Show a high and low value
9	Donut	Like pie chart but for more than one data series
10	Surface	3D chart connecting a set of data points
11	Buble	Location and size can show relaionships - often used in social and medical analysis
12	Radar	Aggregate values of multiple variables; the length of each spoke changes for each variable
13	Sparklines	Shows Trends
14	Others	Such as In Cell charts, pictogram and gantt chart

Figure 274 Suggested appropriate uses for different chart types

Column Chart

This type of chart is used to show variations over time. For example sales of products over a year.

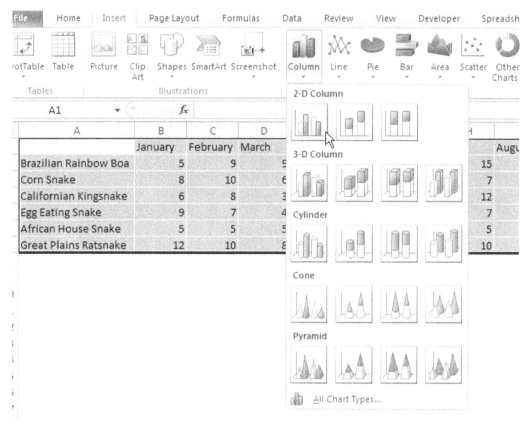

Figure 275 Column Chart

Select the data you intend to chart, then INSERT CHART. In this instance chose the first 2-D column. This will place the chart in the same worksheet by default.

In many situations, the default chart will show the data in an appropriate way. That is why it is the default.

In the figure below, you can see the principal chart elements, of X and Y axis, scales, legend (key), major lines, clear background.

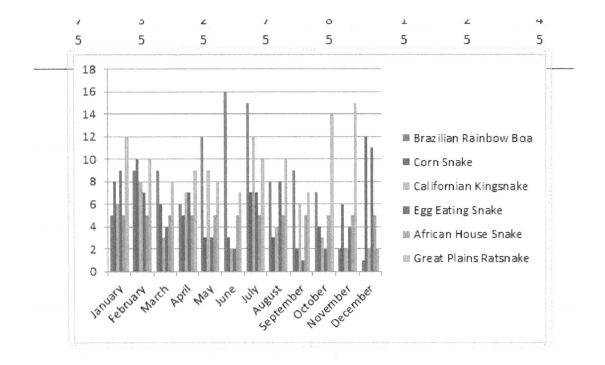

Figure 276 Standard 2D column chart

As you have already seen, these can be edited individually or you can select different layouts and styles. Changing chart layout and styles have been covered previously. It isn't the intention to look at these in detail at this point

You saw in the column chart dialogue box, that there were many kinds of column charts.

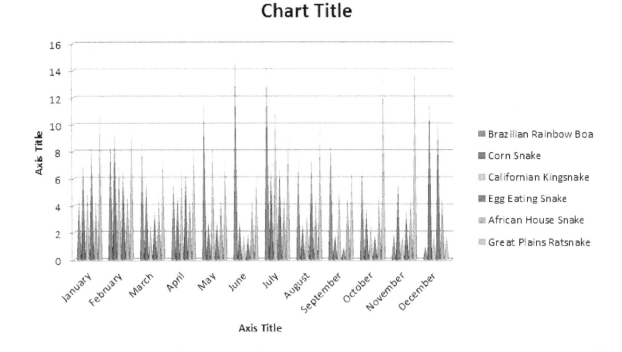

Figure 277 Experiment to find the best chart

The easiest way to find the "right" chart is to experiment with the different options.

A word of caution: - Just because there are options available that you can change, it doesn't mean that you have to. For instance compare the figure below with the simple 2-D chart first shown in figure 272. It is the same data.

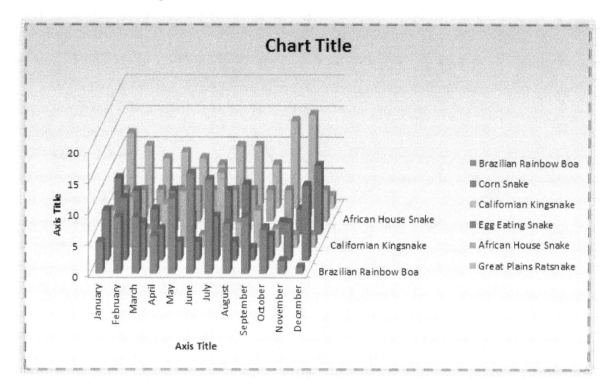

Figure 278 3D column chart

Very often, you will export your chart to another document or to a presentation. Before you commit to a change, always ask yourself if it will enhance your message or clutter the chart and make it incomprehensible.

Line Chart

To help you select the correct chart type pause your mouse pointer over the examples in the chart dialogue box. A callout will explain what it chart is best suited for.

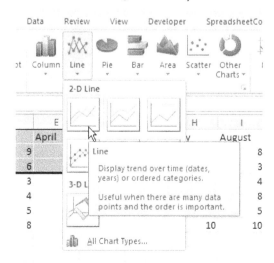

Figure 279 2D line chart showing call out

This type of chart can convey a great deal of information quickly. In this case we are looking at exotic pet sales over a 6 month period. It could equally well be key performance indicators in a project, sales, or mortality rates.

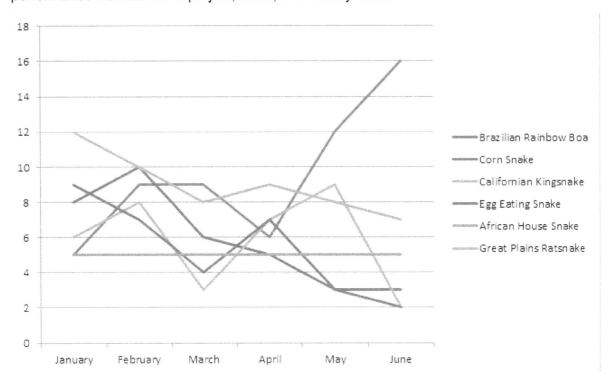

Figure 280 2D line chart

To create a line chart, select the appropriate data; select the Insert tab, then select insert chart.

It is important to note that changes in your data are reflected in the chart. In this instance, sales for the Rainbow Boa have been changed for May and June.

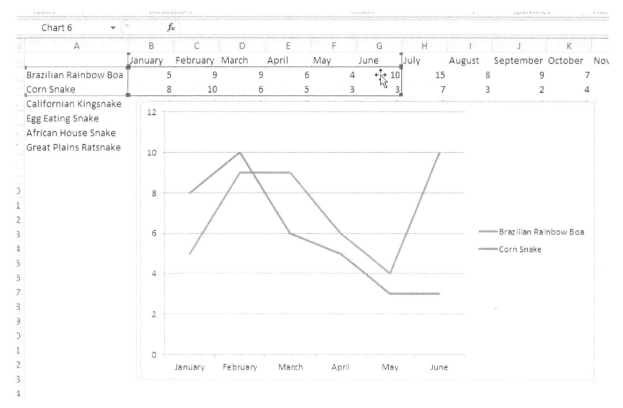

	January	February	March	April	May	June	July	August	September	October	Nov
Brazilian Rainbow Boa	5	9	9	6	4	10	15	8	9	7	
Corn Snake	8	10	6	5	3	3	7	3	2	4	
Californian Kingsnake											
Egg Eating Snake											
African House Snake											
Great Plains Ratsnake											

Figure 281 Changes in your data reflected in a chart

By selecting several of the lines, and then deleting them, this change has been highlighted. If all the lines had been kept, then this would have been harder to see. (compare with figure 276 above).

Pie Chart

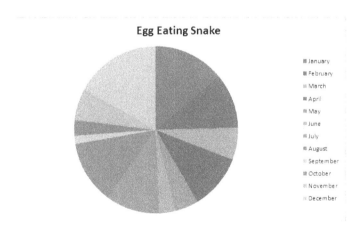

Figure 282 Pie chart showing one data series

This can be used to show parts of the whole, for one data series. Looking at the exotic pet sales for the year, we can select only 1 of the pets and look at the annual sales.

Click and drag along the row for Months (Blank through to December). Hold the CTRL key and drag the row we are interested in (say Egg Eating Snake). If you were interested in the Brazilian Rainbow Boa, you would simply click and drag.

If instead of the sales of one pet over the year, you wanted to chart all pet sales over one month, the process is the same. Select the data you are interested in, and then insert 2-D pie.

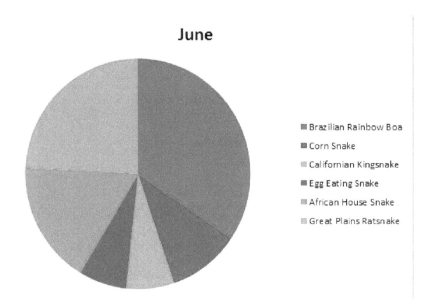

June

- Brazilian Rainbow Boa
- Corn Snake
- Californian Kingsnake
- Egg Eating Snake
- African House Snake
- Great Plains Ratsnake

Figure 283 2D pie chart showing a different data series

In this example you can select the column of exotic pets, and then hold the CTRL key and select the month column of interest (say June).

This chart shows the proportion of pets sold of all sales in June. As the sales can, and probably would, vary each month, comparing different charts in this form may not be entirely helpful. You may have to make the new chart bigger so that the index displays correctly.

To make this chart more informative, you may choose a different style (say type 26) and layout to include % in the pie itself.

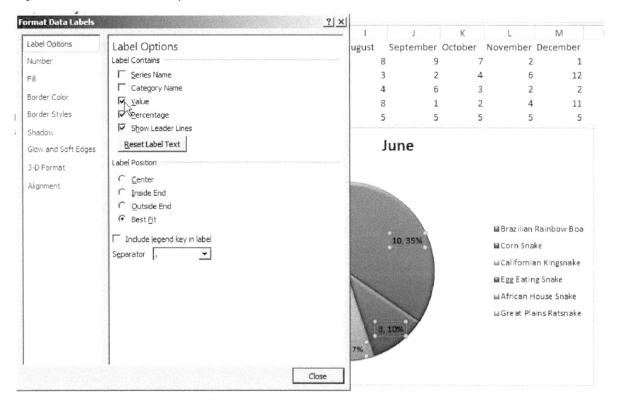

Figure 284 2D pie chart data label options

You may want to change how the data labels are displayed. In this case you will show both the number and %.

Click on any of the existing data labels, and all will be selected. Right click and choose Format Data Labels.

In the Format Data Labels dialogue box, you will see a menu. Select label options. Tick Value. You will see that the label now displays both the number of sales, and the %.

There are many other options you can customise. For instance you may include the category name in the label. This would mean you wouldn't need the legend.

If your data series wasn't exotic pets, but perhaps value of sales made, you could choose number and currency from the Number menu choice.

A word of caution: Make sure you correctly select the correct data series. In the figure below, two blank rows have been selected. Although, they have no values in this case and no category, Excel has created two additional items in the legend.

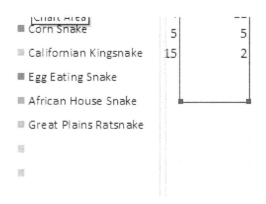

Figure 285 Take care to correctly select your data

This isn't a disaster in this instance. It can easily be remedied. However, it would be best practice to get it right first.

Bar Chart

This is very similar to the column chart you encountered earlier. It will best show changes over time. In this example select only the first two rows.

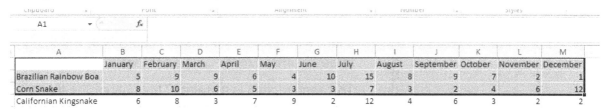

A	January	February	March	April	May	June	July	August	September	October	November	December
Brazilian Rainbow Boa	5	9	9	6	4	10	15	8	9	7	2	1
Corn Snake	8	10	6	5	3	3	7	3	2	4	6	12
Californian Kingsnake	6	8	3	7	9	2	12	4	6	3	2	2

Figure 286 Select data for Bar Chart

It is possible to enter more, but we can keep this example straight forward.

By now, you will see that creating different charts follow the same pattern of selecting data and then inserting the chart.

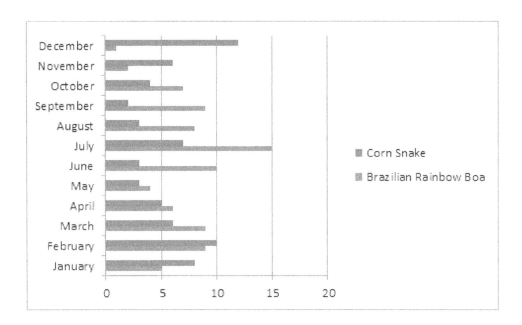

Figure 287 Horizontal bar chart

You will also be getting a feel for which graph is best to display your data as information, and be happy to critically evaluate the graphs you are using.

For example, many people would prefer to read the sales from January to December descending down the page, rather than reading it upwards.

Dynamic Charts, Sparklines and In-Cell Charts

There are three type of chart that you won't find under "Insert Chart" and these are Dynamic Charts, Sparklines and In-Cell Charts.

	A	B	C
.	Month	Cats	Dogs
!	Jan	3	4
;	Feb	4	5
⌐	Mar	6	7
i	Apr	4	3
i	May	3	9
'	Jun	5	4
!	Jul	9	5
I	Aug	1	7
0	Sep	7	8
1	Oct	8	2
2	Nov	2	5
3	Dec	12	11
4			

Figure 288 data for a simple dynamic chart

Dynamic Charts will change as you interactively change your data. If you are following along, you will be trying two types. The first is quick and simple, the second is less so.

Sparklines are a great way of showing trends

In-Cell charts are really conditional formatting, but are a great way to visualise your data.

There are four steps to create a simple dynamic chart. First select your data. In figure 284, it is the three columns Month Cats and Dogs.

The second step is to select Table under the Insert tab. At this point, either select or deselect "my table has headers" as appropriate.

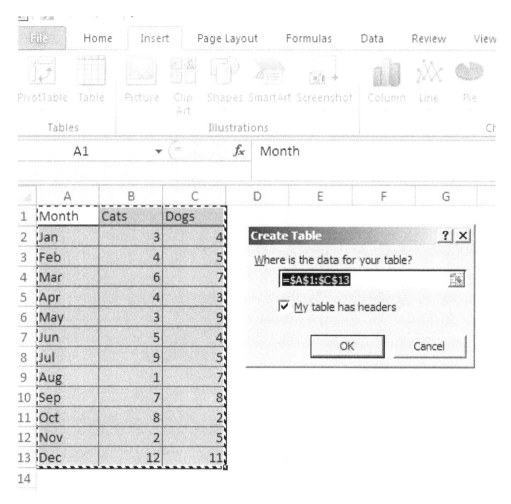

Figure 289 Simple dynamic chart - make data a table

The third step is to create the chart. As you have done several times already, select the data you wish to chart, then insert chart.

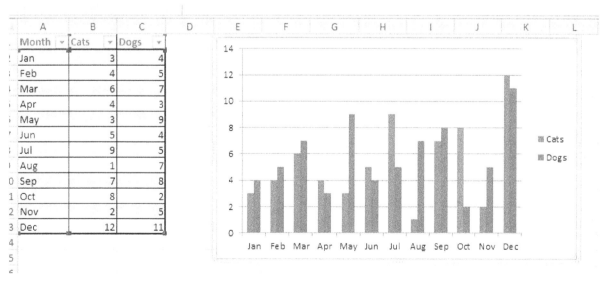

Figure 290 A simple dynamic chart - 2D bar chart

For the purposes of this exercise, it does not matter which type of chart is used. In this case a 2D bar chart has been chosen.

The fourth step is to interact with the data and to see the changes reflected in the chart.

In this example, add a third column, "Fish" and populate the column with the numbers of fish sold. Keep the numbers similar to those sold for cats and dogs.

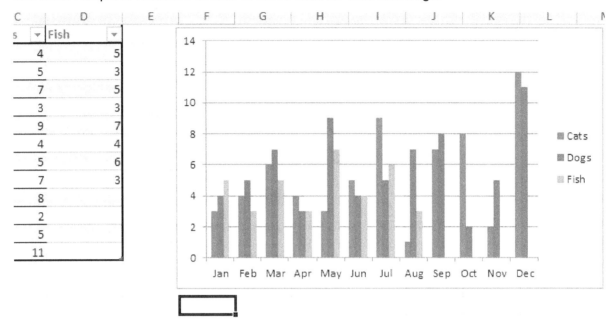

Figure 291 Simple dynamic chart - additional column of data added

Note that the third bar is created as the data is added. Compare August and September in figure 287.

You can make your charts more useful by making them, well, more dynamic.

Take a quick look at your Excel Ribbon. Is there a tab marked "Developer"? If not you need to enable that tab before we progress any further. Click the FILE tab, then select OPTIONS then CUSTOMISE RIBBON. Select DEVELOPER and click OK

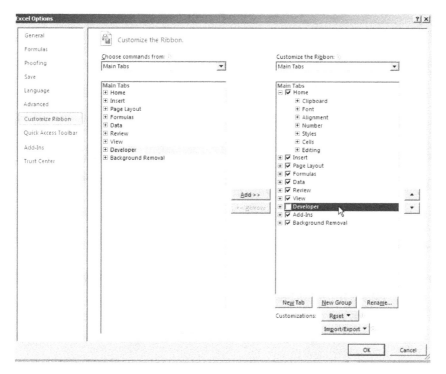

Figure 292 Enable the developer tab

If you share your spreadsheets the others do not need to have this tab enabled.

Create a 5x5 table. Start in A2 and finish in E6. In B2 through to E2 enter years. In A3 to A6 enter four regions (in this case North, South, East and West). In B3 to B6 enter some data.

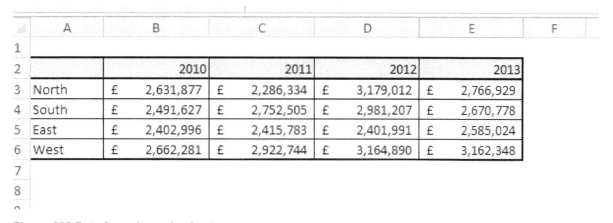

	A	B	C	D	E	F
1						
2		2010	2011	2012	2013	
3	North	£ 2,631,877	£ 2,286,334	£ 3,179,012	£ 2,766,929	
4	South	£ 2,491,627	£ 2,752,505	£ 2,981,207	£ 2,670,778	
5	East	£ 2,402,996	£ 2,415,783	£ 2,401,991	£ 2,585,024	
6	West	£ 2,662,281	£ 2,922,744	£ 3,164,890	£ 3,162,348	
7						
8						

Figure 293 Data for a dynamic chart

The amounts aren't important as long as they are in the same order of magnitude.

This next step is to put the "dynamic" column in, which will become the source of the chart.

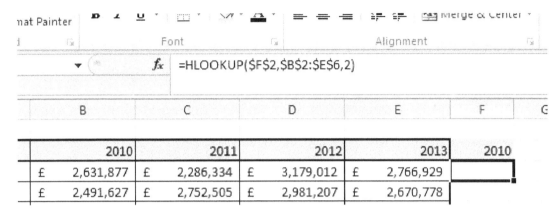

	2010		2011		2012		2013	2010
£	2,631,877	£	2,286,334	£	3,179,012	£	2,766,929	
£	2,491,627	£	2,752,505	£	2,981,207	£	2,670,778	

Figure 294 Enter a column in the dynamic chart

In F2 enter a year from the year row. Any will do, I'm using 2010.

In cell F3 enter this formula "=HLOOKUP($F$2,$B$2:$E$6,2)". For those new to Excel this may look a little daunting. However it follows a standard formula notation. HLOOKUP is a function which looks up values Horizontally. (There is a similar function called VLOOKUP which looks up vertically).

=HLOOKUP($F$2,$B$2:$E$6,3)

2011		2012		2013	2010
2,286,334	£	3,179,012	£	2,766,929	2631877
2,752,505	£	2,981,207	£	2,670,778	$B$2:$E$6,3)
2,415,783	£	2,401,991	£	2,585,024	2402996
2,922,744	£	3,164,890	£	3,162,348	2662281

Figure 295 Dynamic chart - show HLOOKUP formula

$F$2 is an absolute cell reference. In this formula we always want to get the value from the cell F2. When we copy and paste (or drag and drop) it will always look in F2. If we left out the $ then when we copied then in the next formula it would be F3/F4/F5 etc. This would be a relative reference. $B$2:$E$6 is where the data we are going to look up is. "2" tells the formula to look up in the second column.

In Cell F4 enter =HLOOKUP($F$2,$B$2:$E$6,**3)**

In Cell F5 enter =HLOOKUP($F$2,$B$2:$E$6,**4**)

In Cell F6 enter =HLOOKUP($F$2,$B$2:$E$6,**5**)

The only difference is the increase from 2 – 5.

Click the DEVELOPER TAB. Click INSERT. Click SCROLL BAR in FORM CONTROLS (This is the third icon on the second row, and looks like a scroll bar).

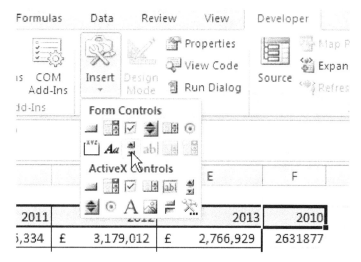

2011		2012		2013	2010
,334	£	3,179,012	£	2,766,929	2631877

Figure 296 Dynamic chart - add scroll bar

Then, anywhere on the worksheet, click and drag. The scroll bar appears. You will be able to resize and change formatting later on.

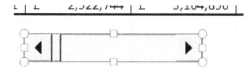

Figure 297 Dynamic chart - place the scroll bar on the worksheet

Right click on the scroll bar and select FORMAT CONTROL

Figure 298 Dynamic chart - Format control

In the control section enter 2010

In the current section (or whatever year you had selected)

In the minimum enter 2010

In the maximum enter 2013

In Cell Link enter f2 – This is the absolute cell reference you used earlier

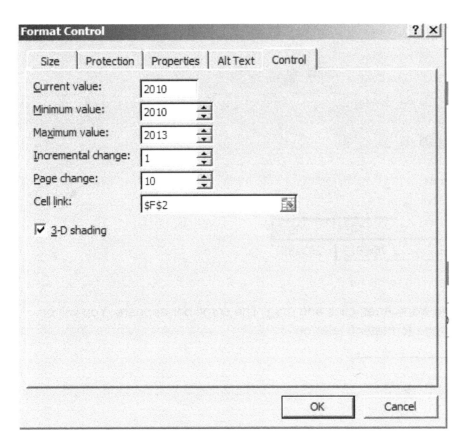

Figure 299 Dynamic chart - format control dialogue box

Select A3 to A6. Hold down the Control key. Select F3 to F6. This is known as making a non-contiguous selection – and you will find it useful elsewhere.

	A	B	C	D	E	F	G
1							
2		2010	2011	2012	2013	2010	
3	North	£ 2,631,877	£ 2,286,334	£ 3,179,012	£ 2,766,929	2631877	
4	South	£ 2,491,627	£ 2,752,505	£ 2,981,207	£ 2,670,778	2491627	
5	East	£ 2,402,996	£ 2,415,783	£ 2,401,991	£ 2,585,024	2402996	
6	West	£ 2,662,281	£ 2,922,744	£ 3,164,890	£ 3,162,348	2662281	
7							
8							

Figure 300 Dynamic chart - non-contiguous selection

Create a chart by inserting a 2D column chart. And place it below the data.

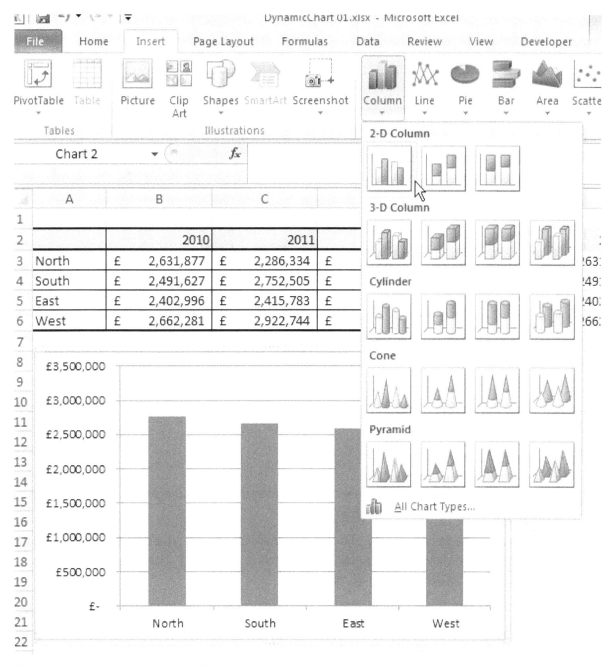

Figure 301 Dynamic chart - use 2D bar chart

Click and drag using the slider bar controls that you added to your worksheet. What you are doing is changing the value in F2. This updates F3 to F6 with the correct data from the respective year.

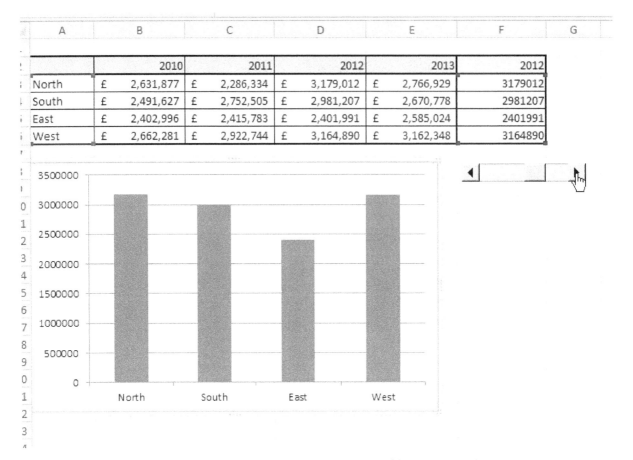

	2010	2011	2012	2013	2012
North	£ 2,631,877	£ 2,286,334	£ 3,179,012	£ 2,766,929	3179012
South	£ 2,491,627	£ 2,752,505	£ 2,981,207	£ 2,670,778	2981207
East	£ 2,402,996	£ 2,415,783	£ 2,401,991	£ 2,585,024	2401991
West	£ 2,662,281	£ 2,922,744	£ 3,164,890	£ 3,162,348	3164890

Figure 302 Dynamic chart - changing the year charted using the slider bar control

In turn this updates the chart. Dynamically! What you have also done is save the need for producing bar charts for each year.

Sparklines are new to Excel 2010. They are a "mini chart" that you can embed in a spreadsheet. They allow you to quickly see trends in your data. There are three forms of Sparkline – Line, Column and Win/Loss.

To follow along with this example, create a worksheet showing sales for a small number of products and a small number of years.

Cell Reference	Contents	Format
A1	Retail Products	Text
A2:A10	Various	Text
B1:L1	Year	Text
B2:L10	Various	Number formatted as currency

	A	B	C	D	E
1	Retail Products	2003	2004	2005	20
2	Auto parts	325,679	325,967	367,651	376,9
3	Furniture	68,939	74,045	78,120	77,1
4	Electronics	74,686	83,033	87,483	80,3
5	Building Materials	303,734	364,037	378,107	337,7
6	Food	417,433	443,633	457,185	463,3
7	Health & Beauty	137,677	145,417	157,468	166,6
8	Fuel Sales	171,887	307,407	344,450	351,5
9	Clothing	147,433	157,888	167,541	167,5
10	Craft and Hobby	77,567	85,137	71,353	71,6
11					

Figure 303 Sparklines - raw data

Select the cell where you want the Sparkline to appear. It doesn't have to sit next to your data, although it makes sense to do so.

Click on the Insert Tab, Chose the option from the Sparklines group. In this instance, you will use Line.

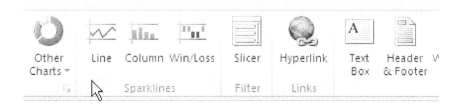

I	J	K	L	M	N
2010	2011	2012	2013		
399,984	401,262	411,165	418,657		
81,123	83,518	-84,994	84,067		
101,501	107,754	110,706	107,086		
331,770	334,736	333,005	306,667		
507 036	536 333	548 734	573 617		

Figure 304 Sparklines - Insert line

You will be presented with the Create Sparklines dialogue box. You must first enter the data range that is to be charted. Some users prefer to enter the range manually, others prefer to click and drag. You then specify where the Sparkline is to appear. In this case it has been automatically entered with relative references.

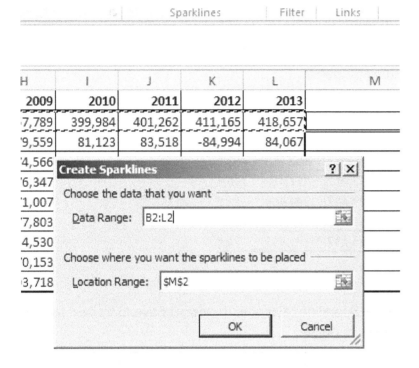

H	I	J	K	L	M
2009	2010	2011	2012	2013	
7,789	399,984	401,262	411,165	418,657	
9,559	81,123	83,518	-84,994	84,067	
4,566					
6,347					
1,007					
7,803					
4,530					
0,153					
3,718					

Create Sparklines

Choose the data that you want

Data Range: B2:L2

Choose where you want the sparklines to be placed

Location Range: $M$2

OK   Cancel

Figure 305 Sparklines - Create Sparklines dialogue box

Click OK to create the Sparkline.

The Sparkline visually represents your data. However, I want to alert you to a potential "problem". It can also aid in misrepresenting your data. In this example I have deliberately kept the column width for the Sparkline the same as those for the data.

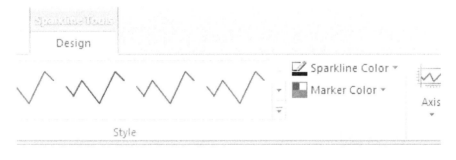

H	I	J	K	L	M	N
2009	2010	2011	2012	2013		
367,789	399,984	401,262	411,165	418,657		
79,559	81,123	83,518	-84,994	84,067		
74,566	101,501	107,754	110,706	107,086		
376,347	331,770	334,736	333,005	306,667		

Figure 306 Sparkline - Warning - column width

It looks like a fairly steep increase.

However, if you create another Sparkline adjacent to it for exactly the same data but the column is three times as wide, the line is much shallower. This may be the message that you wish to convey, that your data demonstrates a shallow and steady increase. The mid way dip appears to be quite minor in the second example, but major in the first.

Figure 307 Sparkline - Column width affects how your data is represented

There is no right or wrong way. Just be aware that just as you represent your data, others do the same. You will have seen trend lines in news reports, TV and in reports you have read. When you interpret them, consider how they are presented.

The Sparkline can be formatted in many ways. All are under the Sparkline Tools Design tab.

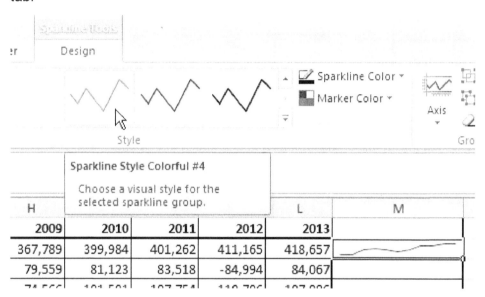

Figure 308 Sparkline - format the Sparkline

The first change we will implement is to change the colour of the line from blue to green. In the Style group select Sparkline Style Colorful #4.

You can change the colour and line width as you wish. Change the colour to green and the line width to 2 ¼.

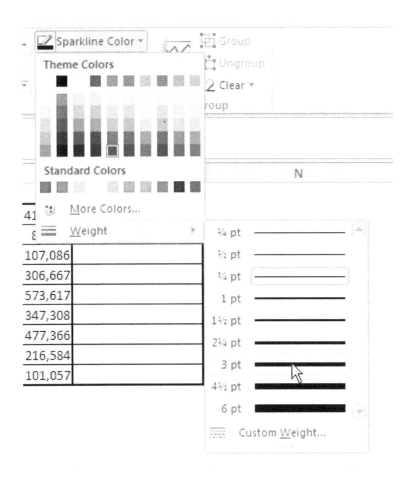

Figure 309 Sparklines - change colour and width of the line

You may wish to highlight points in the Sparkline. In this case you will add a point to the low point. Select the point (s) you want in the Show group.

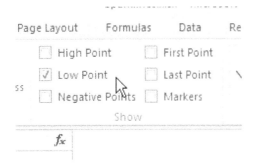

Figure 310 Sparkline - show points

To highlight the marker further you can change the colour in the style group.

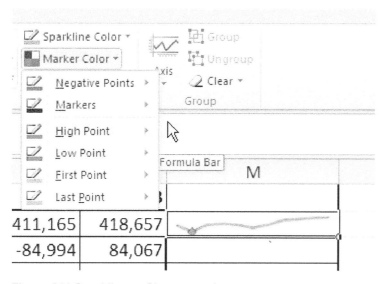

411,165 | 418,657

-84,994 | 84,067

Figure 311 Sparklines - Change marker

To create Sparklines in the remaining cells you can simply fill down by dragging the bottom right corner.

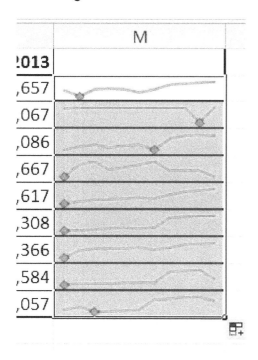

Figure 312 Sparklines - drag to complete

This also copies the format you have chosen.

Earlier you saw how changing the width of the Sparkline cell may change the emphasis of the line. The default axis option is Automatic. This creates an axis that is specific to that cell.

If you wish to compare like with like, then you may want to change the vertical axis to be the same for each spark line.

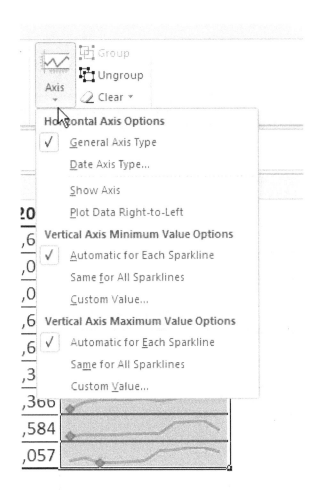

Figure 313 Sparkline - change axis

To do this click on the Axis in the Group group and select Same for all Sparklines for both the minimum and maximum values.

To demonstrate how this will affect the visualisation of your data copy and paste your Sparkline in to the adjacent column. Then format the axis so that they are the same min and max for each Sparkline.

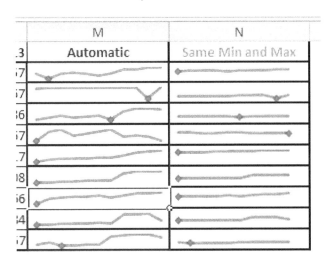

Figure 314 Sparklines - compare changed axis

There is no correct answer, as it is up to you how you represent your data. However, you may want to trust the automatic default setting. Particularly if the rows aren't related. For example in the data used in this section, there is no reason to suppose that furniture sales and electronics sales need to be in the same scale.

You may switch between Sparkline styles. Highlight the cells you wish to change.

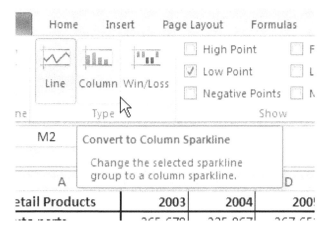

Figure 315 Sparklines - Convert to column

In the Type group, select Column.

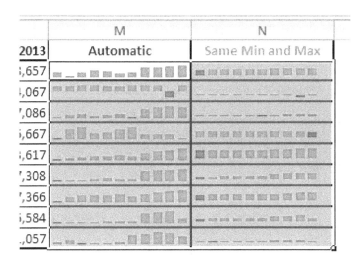

Figure 316 Sparklines - converted to columns

The Sparklines are changed to Columns.

Sparklines are embedded in the background of the cell. This means you are still able to use that cell. You may wish to add text or a formula.

To illustrate this point, you can select the Sparkline cell and enter the formula "=A2". This will enter the contents of cell A2. In this example, it is the product description.

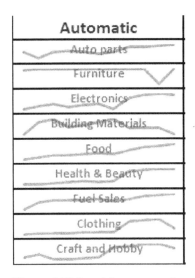

Figure 317 Sparklines - use the cell containing the Sparkline

By dragging you can fill the remaining rows. This formula result can be formatted as you wish.

You can use Conditional Formatting to create chart like contents in your cells. Select the cells you wish to apply conditional formatting to. Then click the Styles group on the Home tab. Select Conditional Formatting.

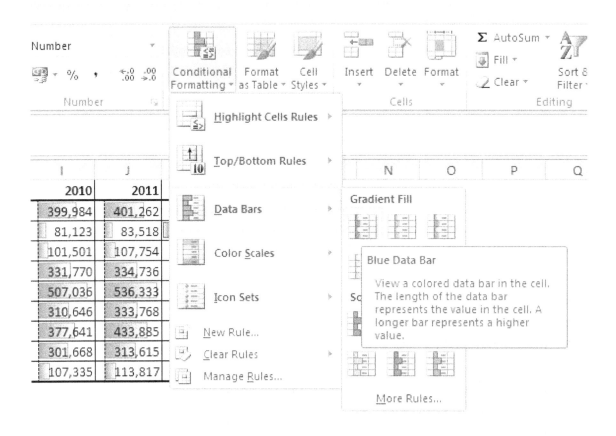

Figure 318 Using conditional formatting as an in cell graph

In this example you will chose Data Bar, Blue with gradient fill. The bar represents the value of the cell contents.

Another option is to select Icon Sets. There are many options to choose from. In this instance select 3 Symbols Uncircled.

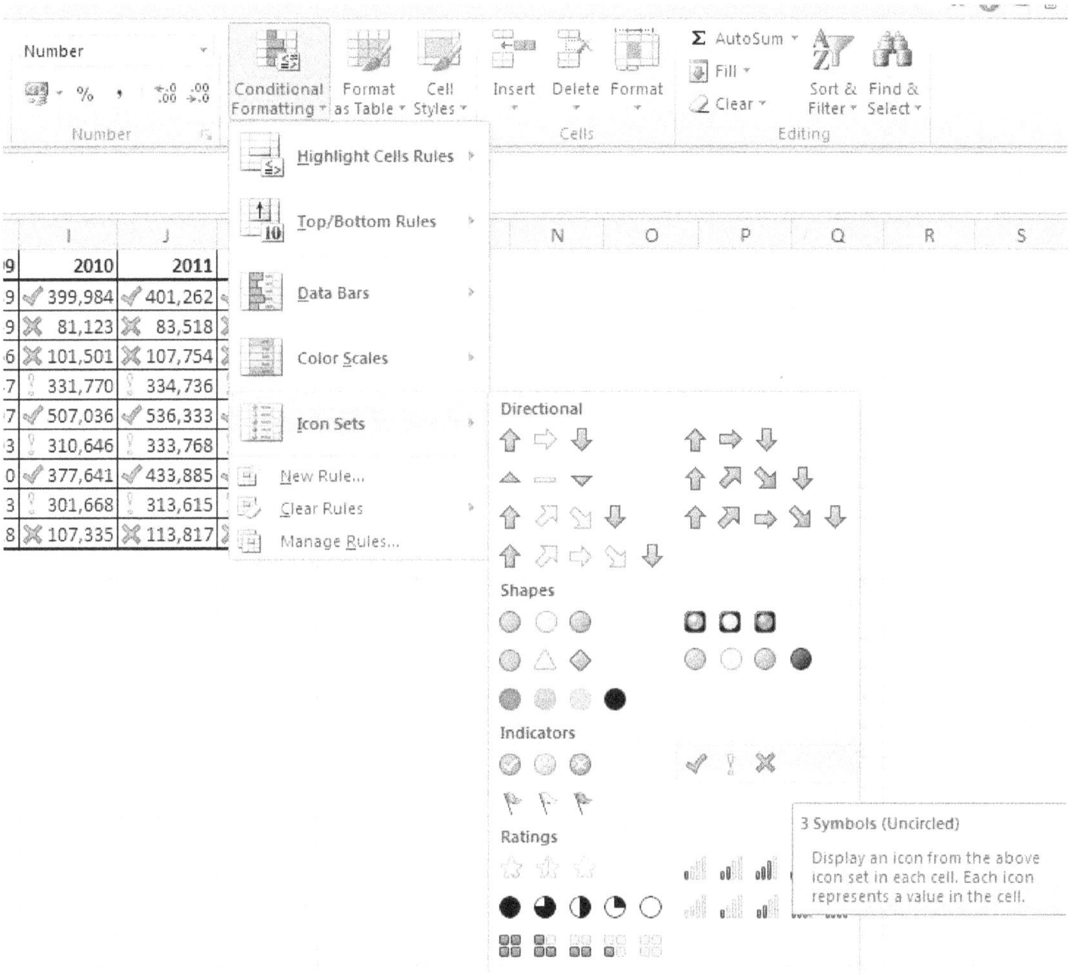

Figure 319 Conditional formatting - Icon Sets

This provides a very easy to understand data set.

Retail Products	2003	2004	2005	2006	2007	2008	2009	2010	2011	2012	2013
Auto parts	365,679	325,967	367,651	376,941	370,269	352,882	367,789	399,984	401,262	411,165	418,657
Furniture	68,939	74,045	78,120	77,138	76,988	77,070	79,559	81,123	83,518	-84,994	84,067
Electronics	74,686	83,033	87,483	80,375	83,877	86,816	74,566	101,501	107,754	110,706	107,086
Building Materials	303,734	364,037	378,107	337,707	348,888	363,833	376,347	331,770	334,736	333,005	306,667
Food	417,433	443,633	457,185	463,330	465,774	475,174	471,007	507,036	536,333	548,734	573,617
Health & Beauty	137,677	145,417	157,468	166,678	180,143	173,630	177,803	310,646	333,768	337,778	347,308
Fuel Sales	171,887	307,407	344,450	351,537	350,770	375,387	334,530	377,641	433,885	451,364	477,366
Clothing	147,433	157,888	167,541	167,583	173,617	178,817	170,153	301,668	313,615	331,633	216,584
Craft and Hobby	77,567	85,137	71,353	71,644	74,610	76,853	103,718	107,335	113,817	111,153	101,057

Figure 320 Cells which include icon sets

However, it raises the question just how Excel knows whether to make a cell a tick or a cross. The answer is that in the background there are rules that are being followed. You can alter the rules to suit you.

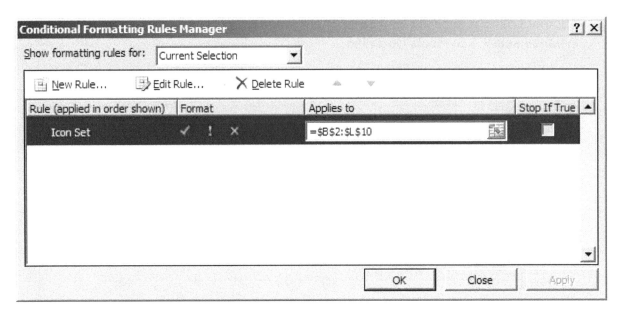

Figure 321 Conditional formatting - managing rules

Select Conditional Formatting, then Manage Rules. Select Edit Rules.

This brings up the New Formatting Rule dialogue box.

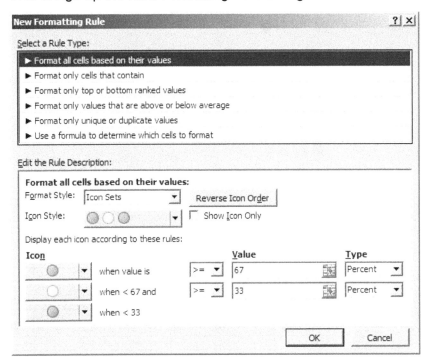

Figure 322 New formatting rule dialogue box

If you decide that the top and bottom 10% need to be flagged as especially good or bad you would change the values to 90 and 10 percent respectively for the Green and Amber. Red will be anything less than 10%. Always remember it is your data and it is your choice as to how you wish to visualise it.

Chapter 5 Working With Data

- Searching your database – filter and use AND / OR searches
- Searching with wildcards
- Using your data in a table
- Advanced Search based on a calculation
- Using a form rather than worksheet view
- Selecting the Top Ten
- Freeze Panes
- Named Ranges
- Hyperlink
- Get External Data
- What If Analysis - Goal Seek
- What If Analysis – Scenario Manager
- What If Analysis – Data Table – Single Variable
- What If Analysis – Data Table – Two Variables
- Create a Pivot Table
- Create a Pivot Chart

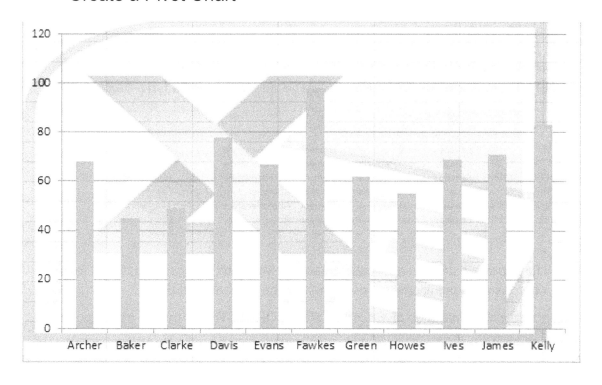

Chapter 5 Working With Data

This is going to be a long section. There is so much to cover and it is where I believe most people will benefit from spending time investigating and using new techniques.

There is no doubt that Excel is at its most powerful when it is calculating. This was what it was originally designed for. However, a great many people only use it to maintain a list. Essentially they use it as a database. Some claim that it is the world's most popular database tool.

So, what is a database? There are lots of technical definitions which we don't need to go in to here. However, in simple terms, it is a list of things, or more accurately, a list of related things. These have common properties that can be grouped.

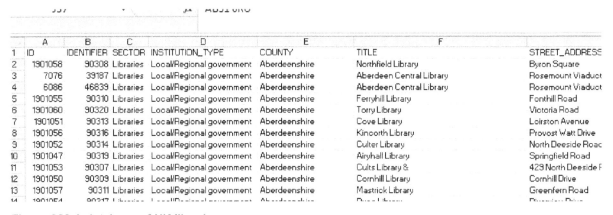

Figure 323 A database of UK libraries

These properties are called FIELDS. A field will have a name and a type. For example in figure 320 you can see a field called ID and it is of a particular type – a whole number (integer). There is another field called COUNTY and that it is of a type - text.

	A	B	C	D	E	F
ID	IDENTIFIER	SECTOR	INSTITUTION_TYPE	COUNTY	TITLE	
1901058	90308	Libraries	Local/Regional government	Aberdeenshire	Northfield Library	
7076	39187	Libraries	Local/Regional government	Aberdeenshire	Aberdeen Central Library	
6086	46839	Libraries	Local/Regional government	Aberdeenshire	Aberdeen Central Library	
1901055	90310	Libraries	Local/Regional government	Aberdeenshire	Ferryhill Library	
1901060	90320	Libraries	Local/Regional government	Aberdeenshire	Torry Library	
1901051	90313	Libraries	Local/Regional government	Aberdeenshire	Cove Library	

Figure 324 Databases have fields

A fully functioning database application, such as Microsoft's Access 2010, will force more rigorous field definitions. Some of this can be replicated in Excel.

A database will be made up of a number of RECORDS. This is the list of things.

So if you create a database using Excel, then the columns represent fields and the rows represent records.

	A	B	C	D	
	IDENTIFIER	SECTOR	INSTITUTION_TYPE	COUN	
1901058	90308	Libraries	Local/Regional government	Aberd	
7076	39187	Libraries	Local/Regional government	Aberd	
6086	46839	Libraries	Local/Regional government	Aberd	
1901055	90310	Libraries	Local/Regional government	Aberd	
1901060	90320	Libraries	Local/Regional government	Aberd	
1901051	90313	Libraries	Local/Regional government	Aberd	
1901056	90316	Libraries	Local/Regional government	Aberd	
1901052	90314	Libraries	Local/Regional government	Aberd	
1901047	90319	Libraries	Local/Regional government	Aberd	
1901053	90307	Libraries	Local/Regional government	Aberd	
1901050	90309	Libraries	Local/Regional government	Aberd	
1901057	90311	Libraries	Local/Regional government	Aberd	
1901054	90317	Libraries	Local/Regional government	Aberd	

Figure 325 A database is made up of a number of records

The Excel cells will contain the data.

To create a simple database, you must decide on the fields that are needed. An example may be a database of movies. This could have Title/Director/Release Date/Actor.

	A	B	C	D	E
1	Film	Director	Release date	Actor	
2	Lady Snowblood Collectors Edition	Toshiya	1974	Kati Meiko	
3	Duel at Ichijoji Temple	Hiroshi Inagaki	1955	Toshiro Mifune	
4	Curse of the Golden Flower	Zhang Yimou	2006	Chow Yung Fat	
5	Kung Fu Panda	John Stevenson	2008	Jack Black	
6					
7					

Figure 326 Database of martial arts movies

In figure 322, these will be the field's titles. This is a particularly small database consisting of only four records. To follow along, create your own database in a new worksheet. Enter these in the top ROW of your spreadsheet. These will be your FIELD NAMES.

Below this enter your data. This is only a small and very simple database. However, it does demonstrate one of the reasons Excel databases are so popular. They are relatively simple to create. Anyone with a basic knowledge of Excel can do it.

Your databases are likely to be more complex, such as a staff compliment and holiday dates, a list of sales by salesperson. The common features are that there will be a list of things that share common data types in fields.

For this next section you will need to look at a more complex database. The example I am using in this next section is from a publically available list of UK libraries. It has been made available using the UK governments Open Government Licence. You may wish to download your own copy so that you can follow along. It is available (as of Jan 2016) from this website https://data.gov.uk/dataset/uk-public-library-contacts-14032012. Please note this is an external website and the author has no control over availability.

Some of the data in the spreadsheet has been changed, so don't rely upon the results if you are trying to find somewhere to borrow a book from.

The first thing I prefer to do is to make it more readable. I recommend making the titles stand out by changing the background of the field names and also I put borders around the cells. Finally, I prefer to freeze panes at A2. This way I find it easier to scroll through the database.

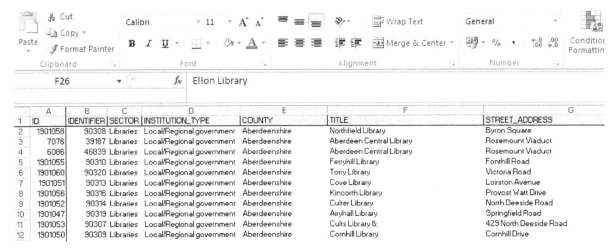

	A	B	C	D	E	F	G
1	ID	IDENTIFIER	SECTOR	INSTITUTION_TYPE	COUNTY	TITLE	STREET_ADDRESS
2	1901058	90308	Libraries	Local/Regional government	Aberdeenshire	Northfield Library	Byron Square
3	7076	39187	Libraries	Local/Regional government	Aberdeenshire	Aberdeen Central Library	Rosemount Viaduct
4	6086	46839	Libraries	Local/Regional government	Aberdeenshire	Aberdeen Central Library	Rosemount Viaduct
5	1901055	90310	Libraries	Local/Regional government	Aberdeenshire	Ferryhill Library	Fonthill Road
6	1901060	90320	Libraries	Local/Regional government	Aberdeenshire	Torry Library	Victoria Road
7	1901051	90313	Libraries	Local/Regional government	Aberdeenshire	Cove Library	Loirston Avenue
8	1901056	90316	Libraries	Local/Regional government	Aberdeenshire	Kincorth Library	Provost Watt Drive
9	1901052	90314	Libraries	Local/Regional government	Aberdeenshire	Culter Library	North Deeside Road
10	1901047	90319	Libraries	Local/Regional government	Aberdeenshire	Airyhall Library	Springfield Road
11	1901053	90307	Libraries	Local/Regional government	Aberdeenshire	Cults Library &	429 North Deeside Road
12	1901050	90309	Libraries	Local/Regional government	Aberdeenshire	Cornhill Library	Cornhill Drive

Figure 327 Formatted publically available list of UK libraries

Searching your database – filter and use AND / OR searches

One of the most common purposes of a database like this is to be able to locate records individually. One way to do this is to search the whole table (aka list or database).

On the home tab, select the editing group and chose the Find & Select icon. Choose Find.

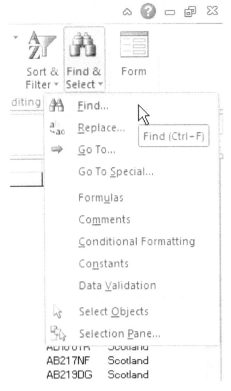

Figure 328 Find a record using Find & Select

NOTE: the keyboard shortcut is Ctrl & F.

Enter the text string you would like to find. In this case, you are looking for "Stockport Central Library". Click Find Next.

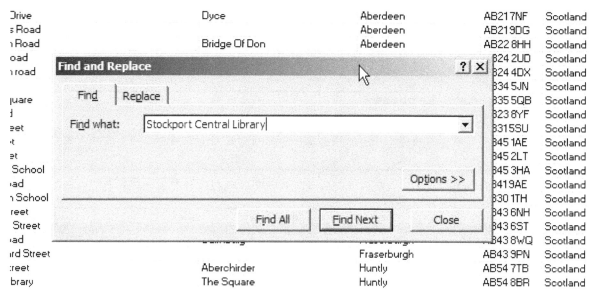

Figure 329 Find - enter a text string

In this case there is only 1 Stockport Central Library

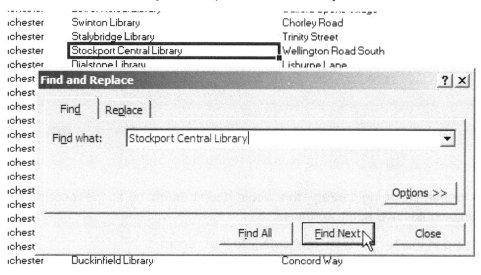

Figure 330 Locating a single record

Now, if you only knew part of the name (in this next case "Central Library") you can use the Find All button. This will search the whole worksheet and provide a list below the dialogue box that is much more manageable to scroll through.

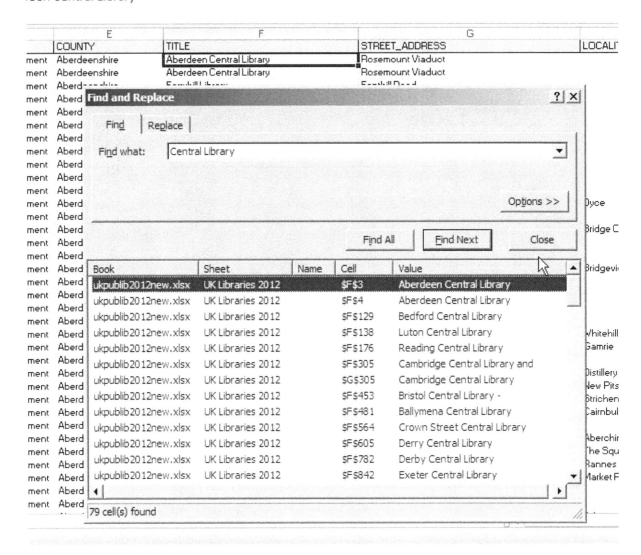

Figure 331 Searching on a partial text

Had I searched for the text string "Library" this would have brought up all the records in the worksheet and would have been worthless.

Clicking on a record in this list will take your cursor to that record.

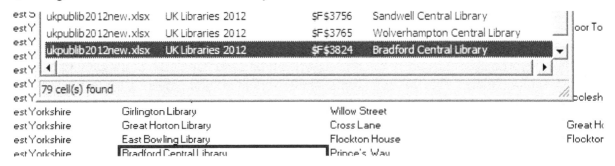

Figure 332 Locate a record - click on an entry in the dialogue box to go to that record

A major drawback of this method includes that you have to already know what you are searching for. I know Stockport is a whole word. If I had searched for Stock Port an error message would have been generated.

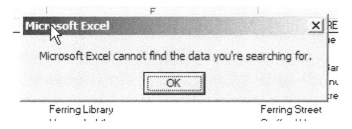

Figure 333 You have to know what you are looking for

This method can't help if I wanted to look for all central libraries in England.

To answer that question we need to apply a filter. To do so, go to the Data tab, and click on the filter icon in the sort and filter group.

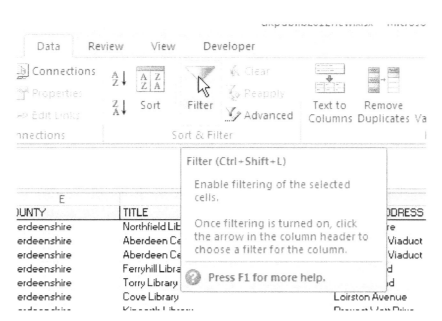

This will allow you to filter one portion of our question. In this case you want all libraries in England.

Figure 334 Filter your data

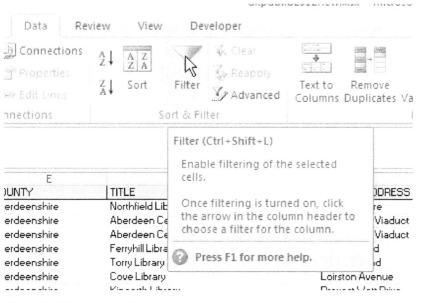

This will hide all records that do not fit your question.

Figure 335 Filter your data

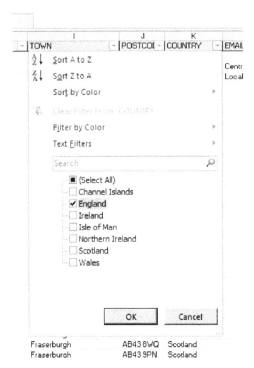

Figure 336 Applying your filter

You can then search this sub set of the data for the text string "Central Library".

So this is a two stage process

- Apply a filter
- Find All

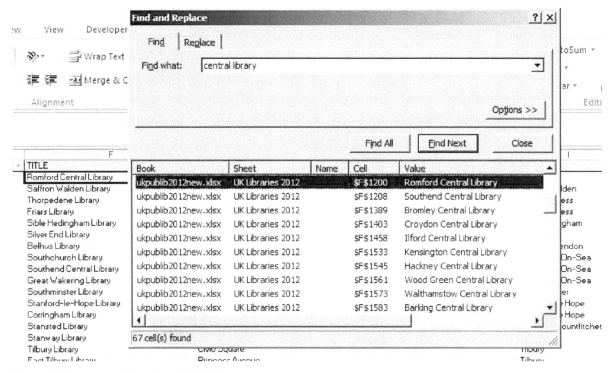

Figure 337 Apply a filter then Find all

It is possible to filter based on an OR filter. In this example, you want to look for libraries that are either in Essex OR in Greater London.

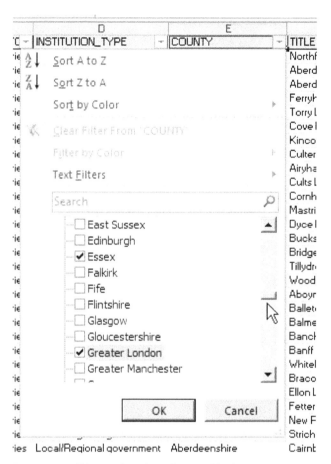

Figure 338 Filter using OR - Essex OR Greater London

This will show only the records for these two counties.

In this next example you will search the sub set filtered on "Essex" for a town called "Rainham". This is an AND filter because it applies to different fields, County **and** Town. This will return two results.

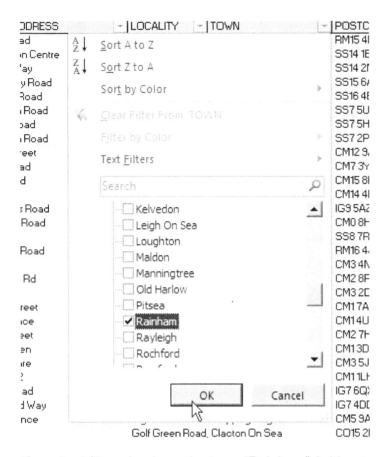

If you had filtered only on the town "Rainham" (without restricting your search to Essex), you may have found more results as there is also a Rainham in Kent. When performing an OR filter you are filtering on just one field, in this case "County".

Searching with wildcards

It is possible to search using "wildcards". These are substitute characters. For example. You may not be sure if the library is in Romsey or Romford, you would search using Rom*. The * means "anything from this position onwards.

? Is a wildcard that means "any character at this position". So you could search for Sand??ch and both Sandbach and Sandwich would be returned.

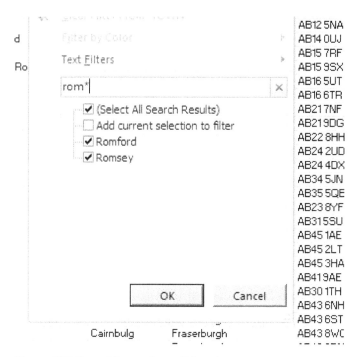

Figure 339 Searching using wildcards

You can position the asterisk at the start of your search. For instance you could search for *ford which would return as results every town that ends in ford. You can extend this to include a search such as B*ford. This would return Bideford, Bradford and Bedford amongst others.

An example of using the question mark wild card could be seen if you searched for "prestwic?" this would return both Prestwich and Prestwick.

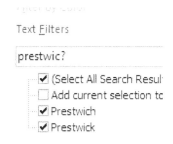

Figure 340 The "?" wildcard

Using your data in a table

So far you have looked at searching data in a worksheet. For many people, this is as complicated as it needs to get. To really take advantage of the power of Excel, you will now look at converting the library data in to a TABLE. This is a series of columns and rows that you can manipulate separately from other data you may have on your worksheet.

To make the task easier in this example, right click the tab; then click on Move or Copy. This will also mean that your original data remains unchanged.

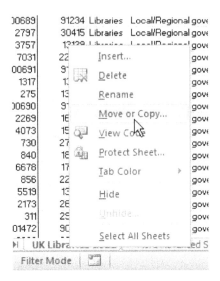

Figure 341 Create a table as a copy

In this instance select Create a copy and (move to end). This will give you a copy of the worksheet you have just been using.

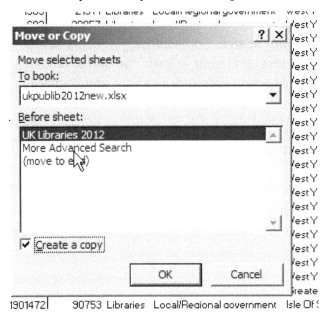

Figure 342 Create a copy of your data in a new table

To further demonstrate Tables, you will also need to click on DATA then click the Filter icon. This removes any filters that are on the copied sheet.

Figure 343 Remove filters on the copied list

Also add several additional lines by selecting cell A1. In the example here, lines 1 to 9 are blank. In preparation for creating the table you are about to use, select and copy the line that has all the field names in (row 10). Paste this in to row 1.

Figure 344 Insert additional lines

Select all the cells that you want to convert in to a table. In this example they are cells A9:N4048.

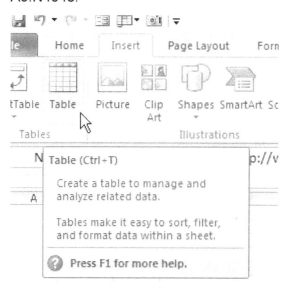

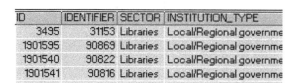

Figure 345 Convert to a table

Ensure the checkbox that My Table has headers is selected, then click OK. Copy row 10 to row 1. You will use this in advanced searching.

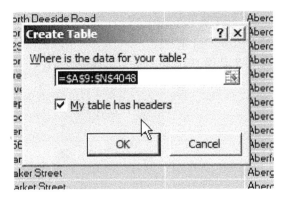

Figure 346 Locate the data and include headers

A table has certain characteristics

- It has a row with field names
- It does not have any blank rows when you create the table

You can add columns and rows as necessary.

By selecting in the TABLE TOOLS tab, you can alter the format of your table to suit. In this instance, using "table style light 1" will give alternating banded rows and provide a simple style.

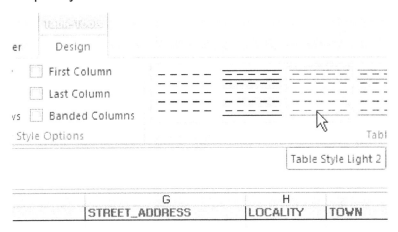

Figure 347 Table designs

The table does not look much different to the original worksheet at this stage. It is possible to search in the same way and to sort as previously shown.

For example, by clicking in the table then selecting Town then choosing to sort on VALUES and in the ORDER A-Z, the table will sort accordingly.

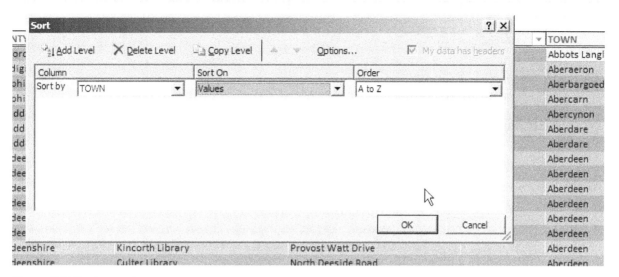

Figure 348 Sort on values

The reason for adding the extra lines and copying the field names is so that you can easily undertake a more complex filter.

Click anywhere in the table, select the Data tab, then sort and filter group and ADVANCED menu option.

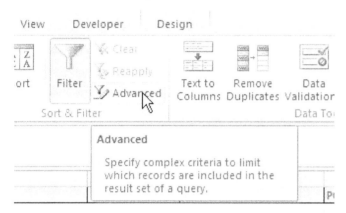

Figure 349 Filter on advanced criteria

The list range is completed by default to be the entire table. You will need to add the criteria range. This is where you will add the items you wish to filter on.

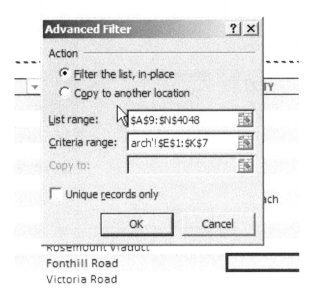

Figure 350 List range and criteria range

For example, you may want to only see libraries in Northern Ireland and Scotland.

A word of warning: at the time of writing Google has over 5 million entries for "excel 2010 advanced filter does not work". So there is a common problem! If you include a blank line in the criteria range, then the filter will not work. So in this example, you may have 6 lines were you can add criteria, if you only use three then 3 is what you must enter.

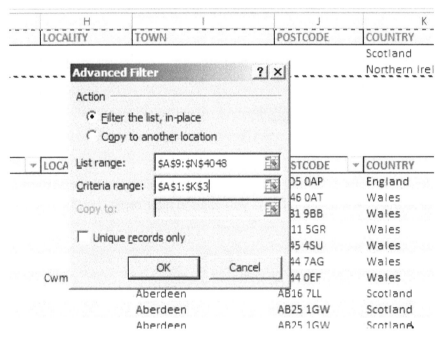

Figure 351 Searching on advanced criteria

In this view you can see how the default criteria has incorrectly completed $A$1:$G$3 yet it should be $A$1:$G$2.

The result returned will have all the libraries in Northern Ireland **and** Scotland. To make it more useful, it will be sensible to sort them in to A-Z or Z-A.

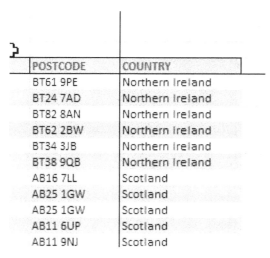

POSTCODE	COUNTRY
BT61 9PE	Northern Ireland
BT24 7AD	Northern Ireland
BT82 8AN	Northern Ireland
BT62 2BW	Northern Ireland
BT34 3JB	Northern Ireland
BT38 9QB	Northern Ireland
AB16 7LL	Scotland
AB25 1GW	Scotland
AB25 1GW	Scotland
AB11 6UP	Scotland
AB11 9NJ	Scotland

Figure 352 Unsorted results from an advanced search

It is possible to use wildcards to filter results. A wildcard is a special character that replaces real characters. An asterisk "*" substitutes for any character. A question mark "?" means any specific character at this position. So *London will return Greater London, London, Inner London and Outer London. Using "Eri?" will return Eric and Erik.

To help illustrate more complex filters and searches, I have included screen grabs of publically available health data. Particularly "Summary Hospital-level Mortality Indicator (SHMI) - Deaths associated with hospitalisation, England: Recent publications" which is available from https://indicators.ic.nhs.uk/webview/. This data is (c) Crown Copyright. Some of the data has been manipulated here and should not be relied on for anything other than to illustrate Practical Excel.

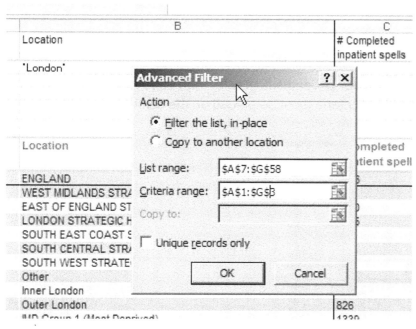

Figure 353 Hospital in patient spells - Advanced search of a table using wild cards

The advanced filter can also be used for AND & OR filters. In this case, you wish to search for those where the number of deaths is more than 25 OR where there has been less than a 1% improvement.

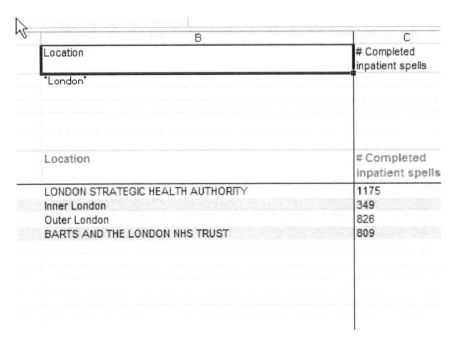

B	C
Location	# Completed inpatient spells
"London"	

Location	# Completed inpatient spells
LONDON STRATEGIC HEALTH AUTHORITY	1175
Inner London	349
Outer London	826
BARTS AND THE LONDON NHS TRUST	809

Figure 354 Hospital in patient spells the * wildcard

C	D	E	F	G
eted spells	Number of deaths	Expected value	standard rate per 100,000	improvement from 2008/09
	>25			
				<1

Figure 355 An advanced OR filter

Enter the criteria on different lines, click on Advanced and make sure that the criteria are selected in the Advanced Filter dialogue box.

To filter out those where the number of deaths is greater than 25 AND where improvement is less than 1% the criteria must be placed on the same line.

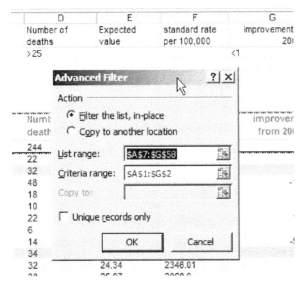

Figure 356 An advanced AND filter

Ensure this time that the criteria range is for one line only.

Advanced Search based on a calculation

You may want to filter your data based on a calculation. For example, to answer the question show all records where the deaths are greater than expected.

In this case, in a new column in the criteria range enter =E9>D9. This will evaluate as either being True or False. Any criteria must give a True or False result for the filter to work. As with previous examples, click on the Data Tab, Sort and Filter Group and select the Advanced option to bring up the Advanced Filter dialogue box.

	Connections		Sort & Filter		Data Tools

f_x	=E9>D9

B		D	E	F	G	H
		Number of deaths	Expected value	standard rate per 100,000	improvement from 2008/09	
						FALSE
		Number of deaths	Expected value	standard rate per 100,000	improvement from 2008/09	
		244	191.76	2270.26	2.63	
		20	11.53	3095.57	3.45	
		29	27.76	1863.79	18.53	
BER		22	15.78	2487.86	-2.75	

Figure 357 Advanced search based on a calculation

The criteria range may not include the reference for the column, so you may have to manually alter this. In this instance it will be to change $G for $H. Then click OK.

As with other criteria, you can make this as complex as you need.

	Sort & Filter			Data Tools	

D	E	F	G	H
Number of deaths	Expected value	standard rate per 100,000	improvement from 2008/09	
		>0.1		TRUE
Number of deaths	Expected value	standard rate per 100,000	improvement from 2008/09	
244	191.76	2270.26	2.63	
20	11.53	3095.57	3.45	
29	27.76	1863.79	18.53	
22	17.91	2191.42	5.26	
32	25.29	2257.53	0.32	
22	22.26	1762.93	18.97	

Figure 358 Showing where there has been an improvement in mortality

For example, if you wish to filter only those where the death rate is less than expected AND where there has been an improvement on the previous year change the criteria and make sure your information in the Advanced Filter dialogue box is correct.

Using a form rather than worksheet view

If you are using Excel 2010 as a database, you may find the worksheet format cumbersome, and would prefer to use a form. You have to add the command to the Quick Access Toolbar

As a quick reminder of how to do this you will need to click on the drop down arrow next to the toolbar, Customise Quick Access Toolbar menu will appear and select More Commands.

Figure 359 Add Form to Quick Access Toolbar

The Excel Options dialogue box allows you to choose commands from All Commands. Scroll to Forms, click Add>>>. Then click OK. A form icon will now be included in the quick access toolbar.

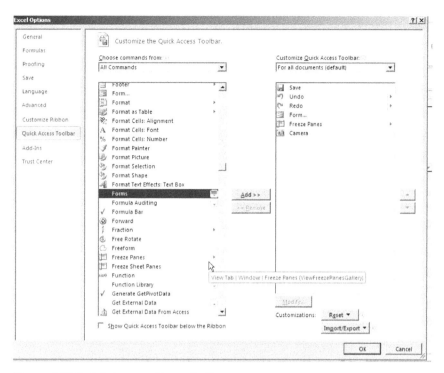

Figure 360 Quick Access Bar – Options

Click in the data that you wish to view (you may have several tables on your worksheet) then click the form icon you have just placed in the quick access toolbar.

This will allow you to scroll through the records rather than scrolling down the worksheet. It will also allow you to add or delete a record.

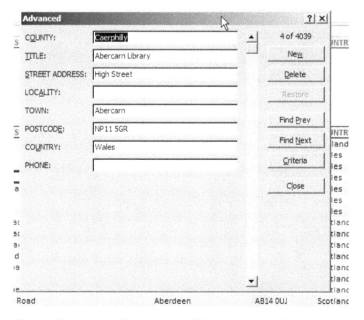

Figure 361 Using a form to scroll through records

You can use the form to search your records. Click on criteria and enter your search requirements. Click Find Next and you will be taken to the first record that meets that particular criteria.

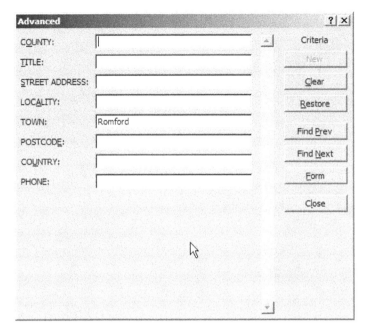

Figure 362 Using form to search records

Find Next will take you to the next record and so on.

Selecting the Top Ten

Often, when filtering data you just want to review the "top ten" items. Excel provides an easy way to do this. On a filtered table, click the down arrow of the column you wish to filter.

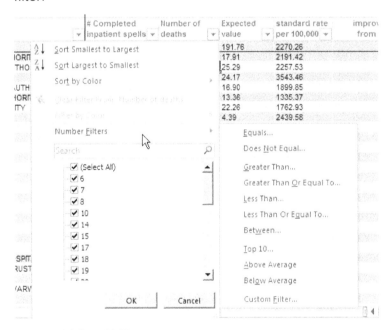

Figure 363 Top 10 filter

Then click Number Filters and select the filter you wish to use.

As you can see from the screen shot it is easy to customise to suit your requirements.

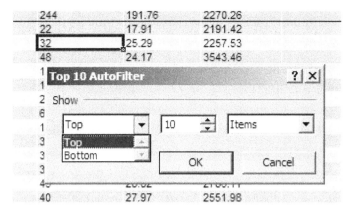

Figure 364 Customise the Top 10 AutoFilter

Using the custom filter you can be even more specific.

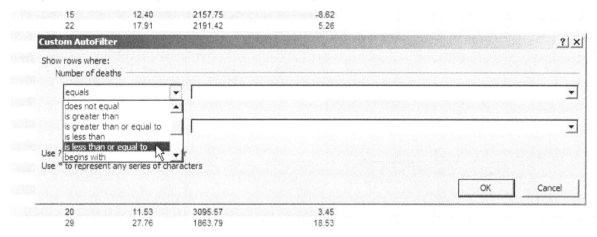

Figure 365 Custom AutoFilter

There is also an equivalent text filter.

Freeze Panes

Using Excel with a large number of records, it is very helpful to keep the column headings in view as you scroll. You Freeze the panes. This means that below and to the right of a selected cell, you can scroll while keeping row and column headings visible.

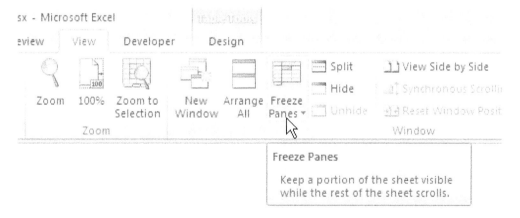

Figure 366 Freeze panes

This is available from View – Window – Freeze Panes. You will have already seen this in use in this example.

To make it easier for myself, I have added the freeze panes option available on my Quick Access Toolbar so I can toggle the function on and off. I recommend that you do the same.

Named Ranges

Working in Excel can be made much easier by using NAMED RANGES – this is one or more cells that you have given a name to. It makes for better understanding if your formula is written say =$C$5*SalesTax. Using a named range is particularly useful if the cell represents a variable that can change. For example a change in VAT from 17.5% to 20.0%.

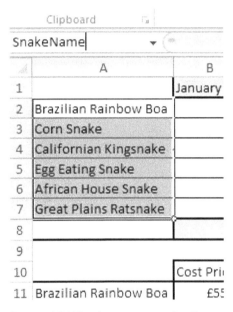

Figure 367 Naming a range of cells

The simplest way to create a named range is to highlight the cell you want to name and then type the name in the Name Box.

It often makes sense to have a single cell as a Named Range. For example, the formula =SUM(b11*ProfitMargin) makes it more readable than =sum(b11*b18).

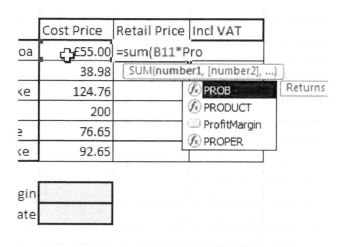

	Cost Price	Retail Price	Incl VAT
oa	£55.00	=sum(B11*Pro	
	38.98		
ke	124.76		
	200		
ə	76.65		
ke	92.65		

gin

ate

Figure 368 A range of one cell

Notice as the named range is added, Excel helpfully adds a short cut.

There are rules to naming a range. It can be a combination of up to 255 characters, upper and lower case, punctuation and numbers. It can't contain spaces or cell references. So ProfitMargin and Profit_Margin are valid but Profit Margin isn't.

To go directly to the named range click on the down arrow on the right hand of the Name Box.

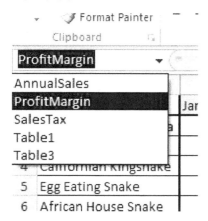

This is particularly helpful in a complex spreadsheet.

You can also name a range by using the New Name Dialogue Box.

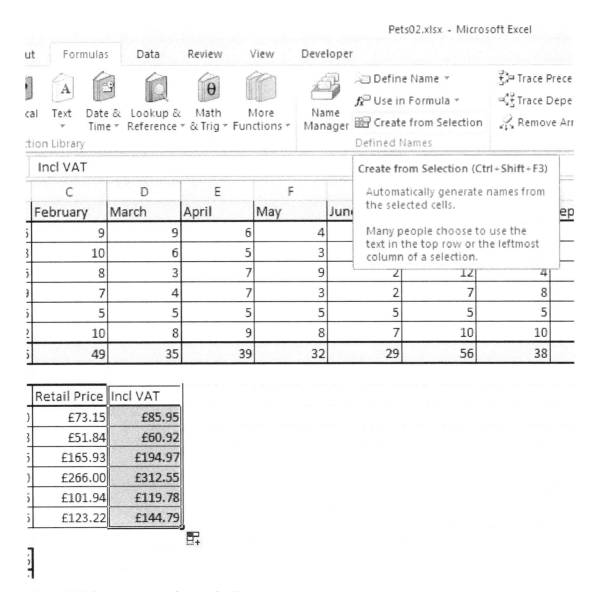

	C	D	E	F				ep
	February	March	April	May	June			
5	9	9	6	4				
3	10	6	5	3				
5	8	3	7	9	2	12	4	
)	7	4	7	3	2	7	8	
5	5	5	5	5	5	5	5	
2	10	8	9	8	7	10	10	
5	49	35	39	32	29	56	38	

	Retail Price	Incl VAT
)	£73.15	£85.95
3	£51.84	£60.92
5	£165.93	£194.97
)	£266.00	£312.55
5	£101.94	£119.78
5	£123.22	£144.79

Figure 369 Create a name from selection

Select the cells you wish to name. Click on the Formula tab and Create from Selection.

Excel will create the named range from the top row as long as it meets the criteria for a named range.

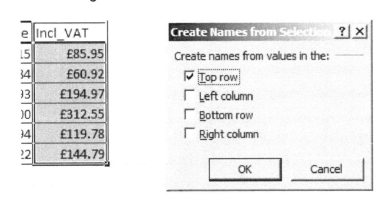

Figure 370 Creating a name from values

If there is a space then Excel will try to create the name by inserting an underscore.

You can see this in action by selecting cells and click Define Name on the Formulas tab.

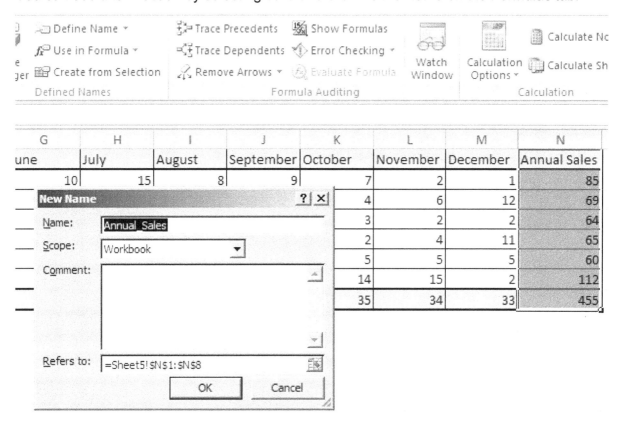

Figure 371 Define a new range name

Clicking the Name Manager icon enables you to create New, Edit or Delete any of the named ranges and to change the scope of any of your named ranges.

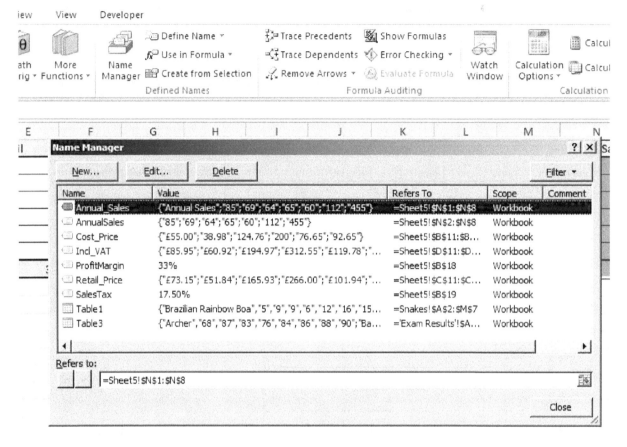

Figure 372 Name manager

Hyperlink

It is often useful to add a hyperlink to records in your data base. A hyperlink is the familiar website like link that on clicking redirects you to either another location (on your worksheet or even another document) or to a web page.

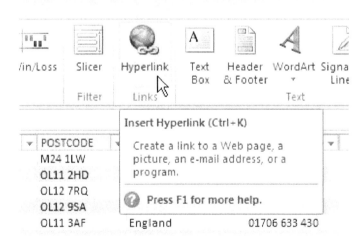

Figure 373 Insert a hyperlink

To add a hyperlink you can select the Insert tab and then click on the Hyperlink icon.

It is often easier to use a keyboard command, in this case Ctrl+K. Both bring up the Insert Hyperlink dialogue box.

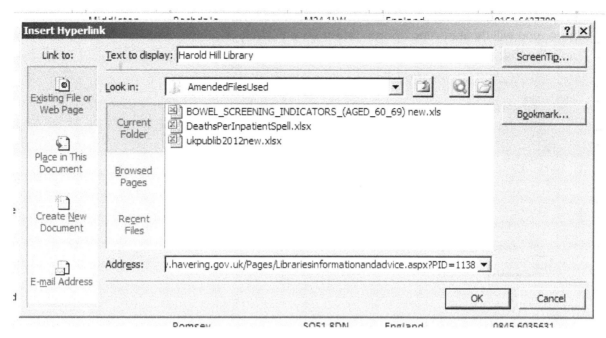

Figure 374 Insert hyperlink dialogue box

Type in the location of the hyperlink in the Address box and then click OK. The selected text will be underlined like any other link.

It is also easy to put a hyperlink to another place in the existing document. You can either choose a named range or use a cell reference.

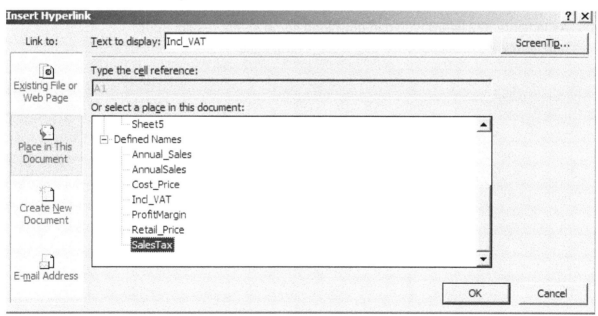

Figure 375 Hyperlink to a location in a document

Get External Data

You can have Excel automatically import data and update it regularly (depending upon your source).

All you need to know first is where your data is coming from. In the example shown here, you will be importing sports data from a publicly available website. It could be from any site that displays data in a table or from a SQL database.

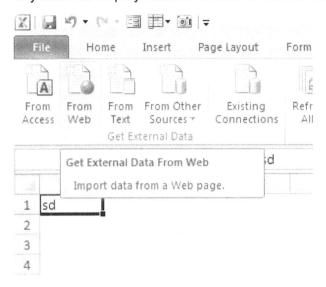

Figure 376 Get external data from the web

You may want to down load share prices or currency prices, and have these automatically updated by Excel. The process is very similar wherever you get your data from.

Go to the DATA tab and select the From Web icon in the Get External Data group.

As in figure 372 below, you can download some sports results from http://www.sfstats.net/soccer/leagues/3_Premiership

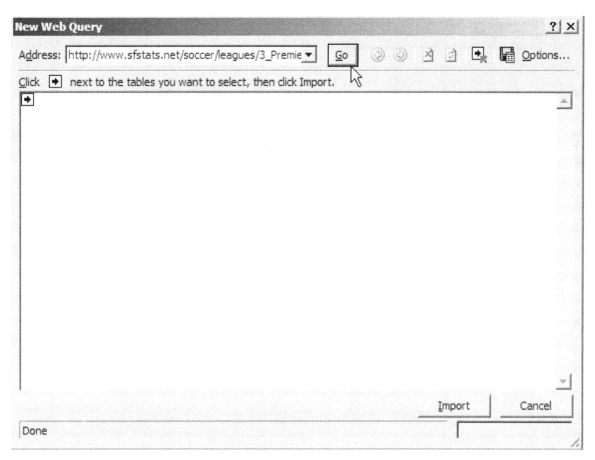

Figure 377 New Web Query

Either copy and paste the URL from the website, or type it in. Click GO.

The dialogue box acts as a mini web browser. The yellow square with an arrow indicates where there is a table from which Excel can download data.

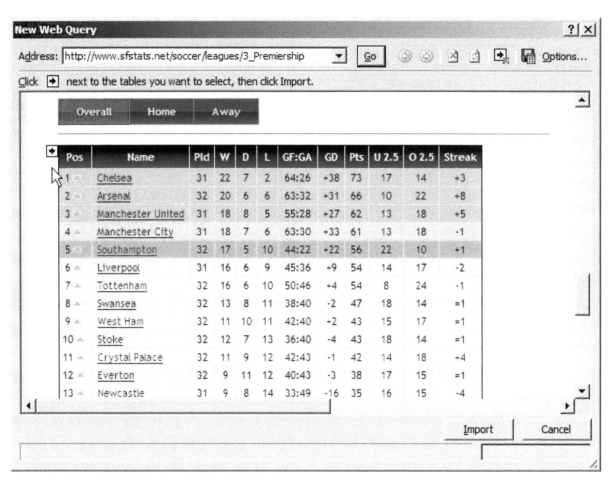

Figure 378 Select the specific table to download

By clicking the Options icon you will be able to choose how your data will be copied.

Figure 379 Web query options

Selecting None will copy only the data and headings.

Click Import and the Import Data dialogue appears. Allowing you to specify where you want the table of data to be imported to.

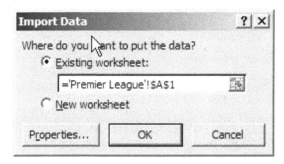

Figure 380 Specify where to import the data to

To open the External Data Range Properties, click the Properties button.

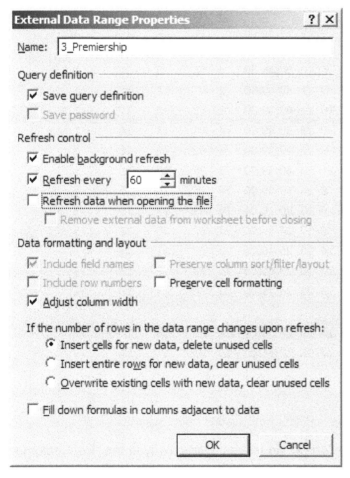

Figure 381 External data range properties

This allows you to specify how often the data is refreshed and what to do if the refreshed data is a different size to the original downloaded data. In this example, the data won't change very quickly. If you needed to keep a watch on, say, share prices or currency conversion rates, then you could set it to update every minute. You have a great deal of flexibility on how your data is treated.

As you can see in figure 377, with the default settings, there can be some issues with the downloaded data. You may have to edit your download before working with it.

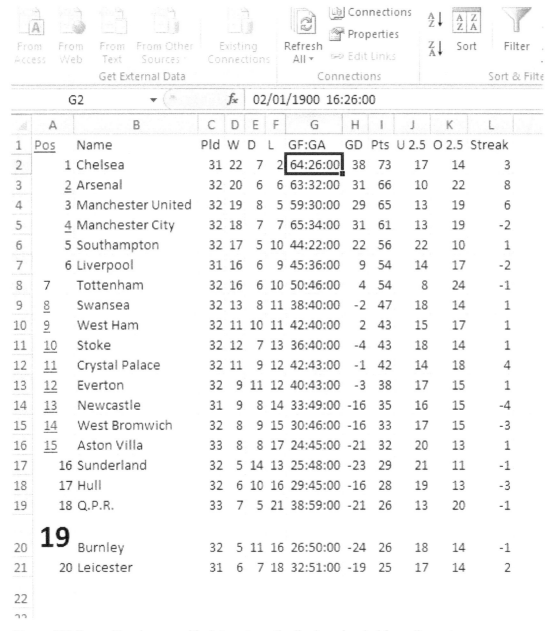

	A	B	C	D	E	F	G	H	I	J	K	L
1	Pos	Name	Pld	W	D	L	GF:GA	GD	Pts	U 2.5	O 2.5	Streak
2	1	Chelsea	31	22	7	2	64:26:00	38	73	17	14	3
3	2	Arsenal	32	20	6	6	63:32:00	31	66	10	22	8
4	3	Manchester United	32	19	8	5	59:30:00	29	65	13	19	6
5	4	Manchester City	32	18	7	7	65:34:00	31	61	13	19	-2
6	5	Southampton	32	17	5	10	44:22:00	22	56	22	10	1
7	6	Liverpool	31	16	6	9	45:36:00	9	54	14	17	-2
8	7	Tottenham	32	16	6	10	50:46:00	4	54	8	24	-1
9	8	Swansea	32	13	8	11	38:40:00	-2	47	18	14	1
10	9	West Ham	32	11	10	11	42:40:00	2	43	15	17	1
11	10	Stoke	32	12	7	13	36:40:00	-4	43	18	14	1
12	11	Crystal Palace	32	11	9	12	42:43:00	-1	42	14	18	4
13	12	Everton	32	9	11	12	40:43:00	-3	38	17	15	1
14	13	Newcastle	31	9	8	14	33:49:00	-16	35	16	15	-4
15	14	West Bromwich	32	8	9	15	30:46:00	-16	33	17	15	-3
16	15	Aston Villa	33	8	8	17	24:45:00	-21	32	20	13	1
17	16	Sunderland	32	5	14	13	25:48:00	-23	29	21	11	-1
18	17	Hull	32	6	10	16	29:45:00	-16	28	19	13	-3
19	18	Q.P.R.	33	7	5	21	38:59:00	-21	26	13	20	-1
20	19	Burnley	32	5	11	16	26:50:00	-24	26	18	14	-1
21	20	Leicester	31	6	7	18	32:51:00	-19	25	17	14	2
22												

Figure 382 Formatting issues with data automatically downloaded from the web

In this instance there are some minor formatting issues. Particularly in the "Pos" column. This can be prevented by downloading in to a new or previously unformatted worksheet.

However take note of how the Goals For and Goals Against are displayed. In the original table Chelsea scored 64, but had 26 scored against them. It was displayed as GF:GA - 64:26.

Easy for a human to interpret, but not so easy for Excel, this has set it to be 64 hours 26 minutes and no seconds past the start of 1900! This is the way Excel formats times, and it has defaulted to the "start" of Excel time.

It would be tremendously unfair to leave you with this uncorrected.

The answer is

- In column N type this formula =TEXT(G2,"[hh]:mm")
- In column O type this formula =LEFT(N2,2)

- In column P type this formula **=RIGHT(N2,2)**
- In column Q type this formula **=CONCATENATE(O2,":",P2)**
- Then fill down for the remaining columns

What If Analysis - Goal Seek

Excel has many built in tools to help you analyse your data.

In this example, you will see how to use Goal Seek, which is a What If analysis. In simple terms Goal Seek answers the question "what do you have to do to reach this objective". What If is a short hand version of saying "What if I do this"

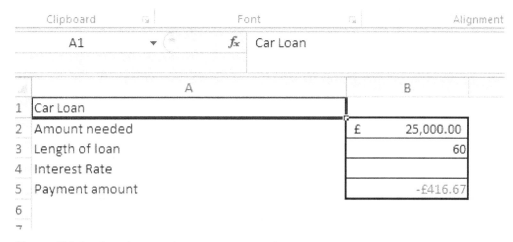

Figure 383 Goal seek example payments on a loan

You may wish to create your own Goal Seek spreadsheet. If so format A1:B5 as per the table below.

Cell Reference	Contents	Format
A1	Car Loan	Text
A2	Amount needed	Text
A3	Length of loan	Text
A4	Interest Rate	Text
A5	Payment amount	Text
B2	25000	Currency
B3	60	Number – no decimal places – this is the length of the loan in months
B4	Blank	Number – two decimal places
B5	=PMT(B4/12,B3,B2)	Currency

This simple example will help you find the interest you need to pay, to make a payment amount of £500.00 per month. At this point, you needn't understand the particular function used, as it is explained elsewhere.

Copy out the spreadsheet as shown, but in B5 enter the following (without quotation marks) "=PMT(B4/12,B3,B2)"

Select the data tab, data tools and click on the What If Analysis icon. Click Goal Seek.

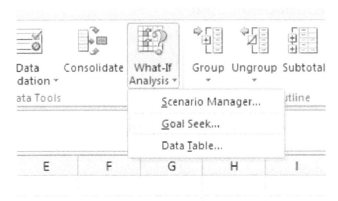

Figure 384 Data tools What-If Analysis Goal Seek

The dialogue box you are presented with allows you to answer the question "If you change this cell to this value, what needs to be the value in the remaining cell". Or to put it another way If you make B5 £500 (the required payment), then calculate the interest rate.

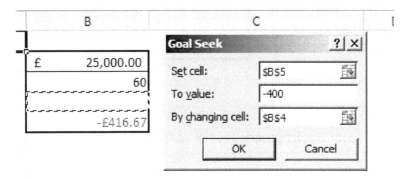

Figure 385 Goal seek dialogue box

Please note in this example the "To Value" needs to be a **negative** number. This is because it is the amount that you want to subtract from your loan. If you forget the minus sign, it will generate a #NUM error.

You are presented with an information box which tells you that Excel found a solution (it might not have done).

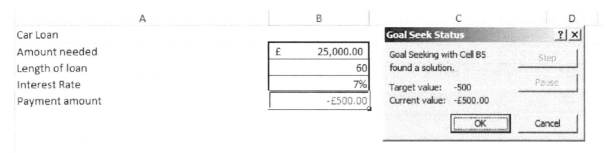

Figure 386 Goal Seek Status information box

In this example, to pay £500 per month on a £25,000 loan over 5 years, you would need a loan with an interest rate of 7%.

What If Analysis – Scenario Manager

There are times when you will want to look at what the effect will be on your data when you change different cell values. It is helpful to be able to store these so that you can keep and review changes. Excel provides this with Scenario Manager.

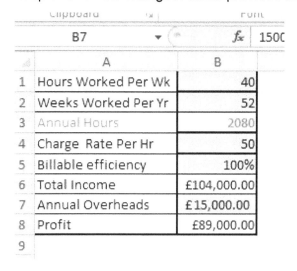

Figure 387 Scenario Manager

In the example in Figure 382, you can look at the effect on how much a contractor can earn by varying the number of hours worked per week, the number of weeks earned in a year, the efficiency of the work and the hourly rate charged.

If the contractor worked all week every week then that would be 100% efficiency. However, in the real world, not all contracts follow consecutively. There has to be time spent finding new business and even dealing with admin.

Create a worksheet with the same figures as in Figure 382.

The formula for annual hours is "=SUM(B1*B2)"; Total income is "=SUM(((B1*B2)*B4)*B5)" and Profit is "=SUM(B6-B7)".

To save a scenario, on the data tab, data tools, What If Analysis select Scenario Manager.

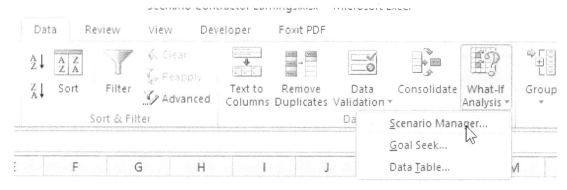

Figure 388 Scenario Manager

The dialogue box will show any previous scenarios that have been saved.

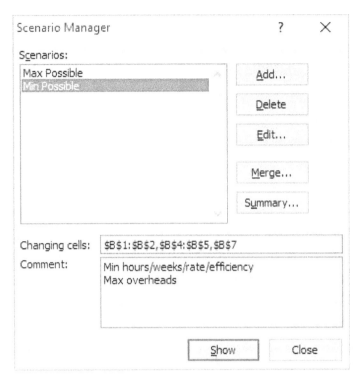

Figure 389 Scenario manager dialogue box

Click Add. The dialogue box will change. Give your new scenario a meaningful name; Select the cells that you want to change.

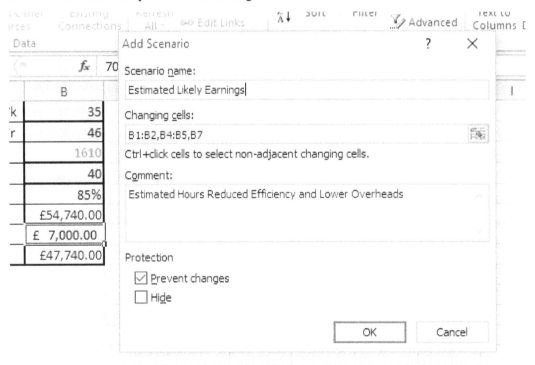

Figure 390 Add scenario

It is good practice to explain what the scenario will do. This is particularly helpful when you return to a spreadsheet after a period of time. Click OK.

Enter the values that you want in the scenario you wish to save. Click OK.

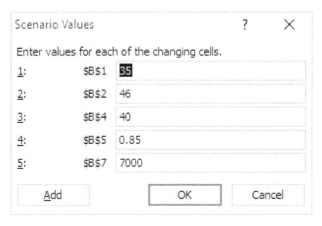

Figure 391 Change scenario values

To call up a saved scenario go to the data tab, data tools, What If Analysis and select Scenario Manager. Then chose the scenario to be recalled. Click Show.

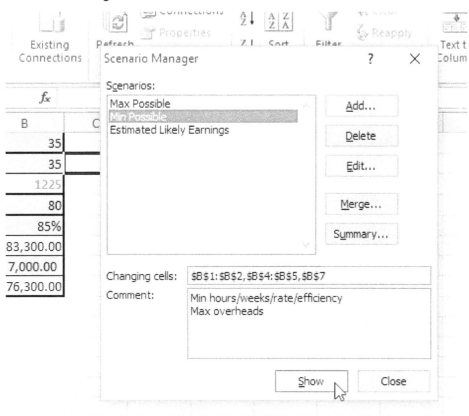

Figure 392 Re using a saved scenario

The results will change on your sheet to those of the stored scenario.

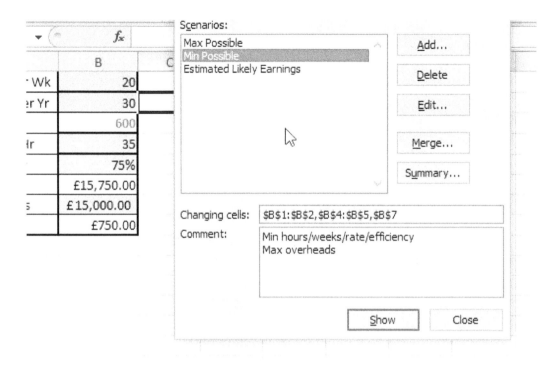

Figure 393 Displaying results from selected scenario

What If Analysis – Data Table – Single Variable

A Data Table is another way of performing a what-if analysis. These come in two varieties, single variable and two variables.

The first example you will see is that of the single variable.

	A	B
1	Cost of equipment	£1,000
2	Cost of making item	6
3	Retail Price (excl Taxes)	25
4	Est Annual Sales	100
5	Profit	£900
6		

Figure 394 Single variable data table

In the example in Figure 389 you will investigate a part time craft business, such as a carpenter who makes children's pull along toys. To start the business there will be some fixed costs such as equipment for the toy shop. There will be a cost of making each toy, a retail price and an estimate for the amount of profit made.

The formula for this is =SUM((B3-B2)*B4-B1). In English this is the retail price minus the cost of manufactured. This then multiplied by the estimate of annual sales. Then with the cost of equipment subtracted.

With the worksheet set as it is, there is nothing to stop you comparing what would happen if approximately 3 units per week were sold rather than just 2.

You could change any of the other variables as well. However, if you want to see what happens when you reduce the cost of manufacture or change the retail price you need a data table.

To set up the data table list the column of the annual sales in an increment of 10. For convenience you can also use the Fill Series within Editing on the home tab

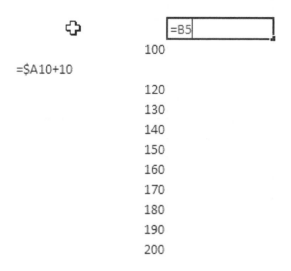

Figure 395 Single Variable data table

The cell directly above the column is left blank.

The adjacent right column has to be headed with a formula. Link this to the profit (in this case =B5).

To create the data table highlight all the cells of the table. Then on the data tab, click what if then data table.

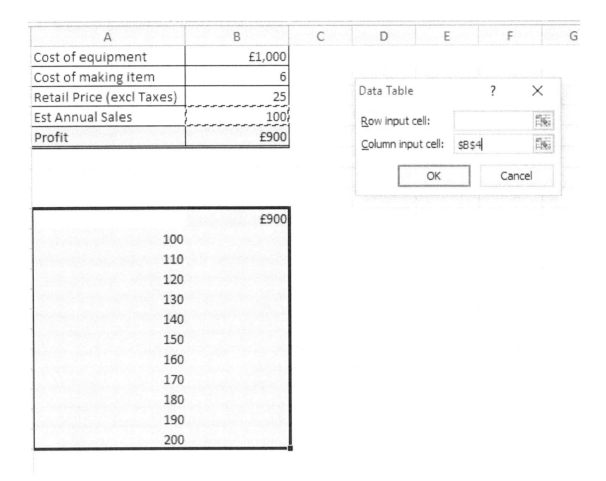

Figure 396 Data Table - enter row and column input cells

The dialogue box allows you to enter row and column input cells. As this table is a column, you must enter the cell reference for the data you wish to change in the Column Input Cell.

It would be perfectly valid to have the changing cells increase in a row left to right. In that case the data would be entered in the Row Input Cell.

An easy way to remember is that Rows go across and columns go down. Just place the variable in the Row or Column.

Click Ok and the table will populate.

	A	B
1	Cost of equipment	£1,000
2	Cost of making item	6
3	Retail Price (excl Taxes)	50
4	Est Annual Sales	100
5	Profit	£3,400
6		
7		
8		
9		£3,400
10	100	3400
11	110	3840
12	120	4720
13	130	6040
14	140	7800
15	150	10000
16	160	12640
17	170	15720
18	180	19240
19	190	23200
20	200	27600
21		

Figure 397 Data table - populated

Place your cursor in one of the cells in the table and you will see the formula for the table. In this case {=TABLE(,B4)}

The curly brackets show that this is an Excel array formula. Now you have a data table it is possible to play with the variables to see how much money the business could make.

For example, the retail price could double, or the cost of manufacture could change.

The table as it first stands allows you to readily see what profit you can earn with increasing sales. For example you can see that doubling your sales from 2 toys per week, to four toys per week will return a profit of £2800.

You can model the effects of changing your costs and retail price.

Add £10 to the retail price, reduce costs by £1 and sell four toys per week and the profit jumps to £5000. Not too bad for a hobby business.

What If Analysis – Data Table – Two Variables

A two variable data table enables you to see at a glance what the effects are of changing 2 variables. In the example here, changing retail price and the quantity sold.

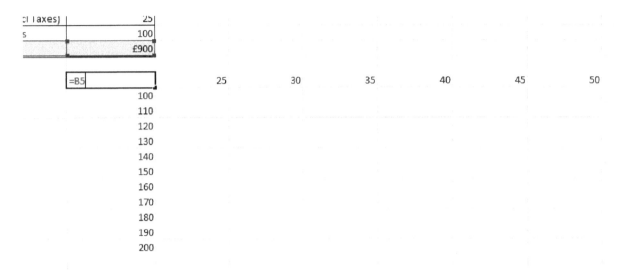

CI Taxes)	25
s	100
	£900

=B5		25	30	35	40	45	50
	100						
	110						
	120						
	130						
	140						
	150						
	160						
	170						
	180						
	190						
	200						

Figure 398 Two variable data table

You start with exactly the same information when creating the one variable data table.

First create your series down (column) starting at your base sale figure of 100. I used fill series to take this to 200.

Then create your series across (row) starting at your initial sales price of £25 going to £50.

The cell in between the row and column is where you place a formula that references both column and row. It is perfectly valid to retype the formula that is in B5 [=SUM((B3-B2)*B4-B1)]. However, for simplicity I like to keep my formula short and just make it." =B5".

Highlight all the cells of the table. Then on the data tab, what if analysis and then data table.

(es)	25
	100
	£900

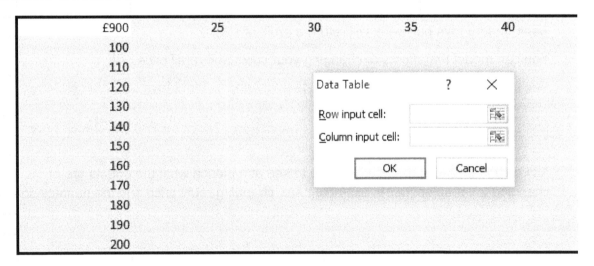

Figure 399 Two Variable data table dialogue box

You get the same dialogue box that you saw in the single data table.

In the Row input cell click in to the retail price cell (B3) and in the Column input cell click in to the Est annual sales (B4). Click OK.

The data table populates. Instantly you can see the effects of increasing sales and increasing retail price.

£900	25	30	35	40	45	50
100	900	1400	1900	2400	2900	3400
110	1090	1640	2190	2740	3290	3840
120	1280	1880	2480	3080	3680	4280
130	1470	2120	2770	3420	4070	4720
140	1660	2360	3060	3760	4460	5160
150	1850	2600	3350	4100	4850	5600
160	2040	2840	3640	4440	5240	6040
170	2230	3080	3930	4780	5630	6480
180	2420	3320	4220	5120	6020	6920
190	2610	3560	4510	5460	6410	7360
200	2800	3800	4800	5800	6800	7800

Figure 400 Populated two variable data table

As an aside, you might think that increasing price will reduce sales. It isn't always the case. It can be reflection of quality. Remember this spreadsheet is for a craft business making wooden toys. Similarly jumping from 100 to 200 per year might seem a lot, but it really is no more than making 4 and not 2 toys per week!

Create a Pivot Table

You may need to analyse data that is in a long and complex spreadsheet. To help, Microsoft Excel uses PIVOT TABLES. These allow you to quickly and simply display your data. They are called "pivot" tables because you can interactively turn your data on its head and analyse it in multiple ways.

Once you have gained a little experience of Pivot Tables, you would normally start by planning how you want your data to appear before you create your pivot. For now, it is best to follow along with this example and to accept the defaults.

This is important - The first step in creating a Pivot Table is to prepare the data. Make sure that all columns have headings, that there are no blank columns or rows, and that the data is consistent in each column. For example, that all are either numbers, or text or dates etc.

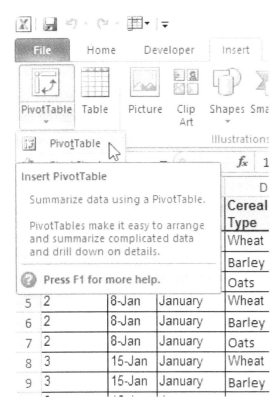

Figure 401 Create a Pivot Table from prepared data

In the example in Figure 396, there are weekly data of volumes of different cereals sold in the UK. You will want to look at monthly totals by cereal type.

To create a Pivot Table, chose the insert tab, tables group and Insert Pivot table.

The Create Pivot Table dialogue box appears, and is pre-populated. You can see the area selected is surrounded by dashed lines.

	A1	▼		*fx*	1	

	A	B	C	D	E	F	C
	Week No:	Date	Month	Cereal Type	Quantities sold in tonnes	Average price £ per tonne	
5	45	6-Nov	November	Barley	32.640	122.20	
5	45	6-Nov	November	Oats	2.305	103.20	
7	46	12 Nov	November	Wheat	62.991	124.00	

Create PivotTable ? ✕

Choose the data that you want to analyze

◉ Select a table or range

    Table/Range: 2015 Prepared Data'!$A$1:$F$157

○ Use an external data source

    Choose Connection...

    Connection name:

Choose where you want the PivotTable report to be placed

◉ New Worksheet

○ Existing Worksheet

    Location:

                  OK   Cancel

			Oats			
2	51	18-Dec	December	Wheat	45.761	139.90
3	51	18-Dec	December	Barley	15.457	123.90

Figure 402 Create Pivot Table dialogue box

Mostly you will keep the defaults. If they are not right, just click and highlight the correct area. Generally, I suggest you will want your pivot table to appear in a new worksheet. Click OK.

The Pivot Table Field List is a slightly more complex dialogue box than you may have been used to.

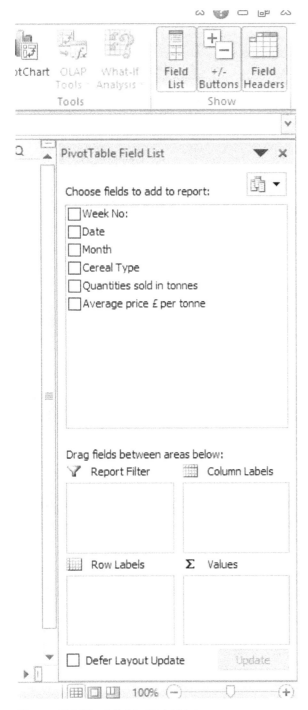

Figure 403 Pivot Table Field List

However, in reality it is very simple. This is where you pivot your data as you are analysing your data. You already know you want to see by month, how much of each cereal was imported. In this case the columns are the Months and the rows are the Cereal Type fields.

Click and drag these to the respective Column Labels and Row Labels boxes.

The $\sum$ Values are where the totals are calculated. In this case you want to know how many tonnes of each cereal were sold.

As you click and drag the pivot table is populated.

You will see that totals for each month and grand totals are calculated.

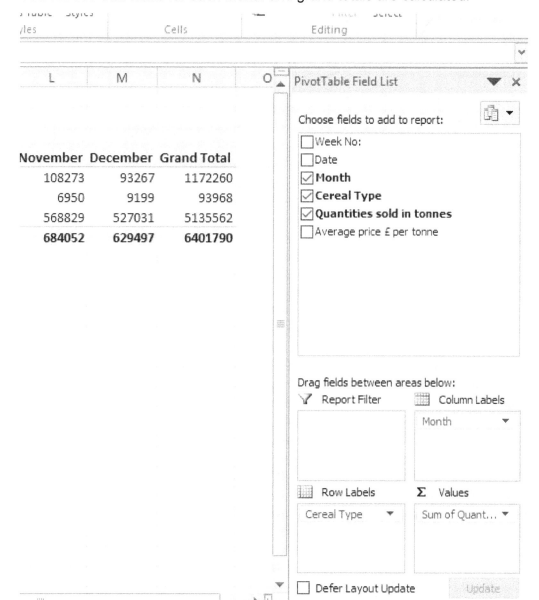

Figure 404 Pivot Table Field List - Populated and calculated

[As an aside, this data is provided weekly. To allocate a month, one technique is to create a "sacrifice" column with a calculated field. In this instance, the calculation in the new column is =TEXT(B132,"mmmm"), where B132 is the field where the week number is and "mmmm" is the format we want to display the month. We could have used mm for the month number, mmm for a three letter month (e.g. Oct).]

It is easy to sort or filter the data in the pivot table. You will be already familiar with the clicking the header arrow to filter. Use this to, say, select just Barley.

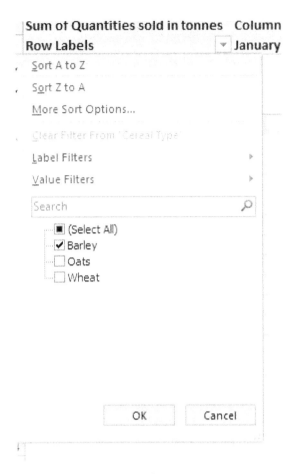

Figure 405 Pivot table - filter

To sort the table, Select a cell in the pivot that you wish to sort on. Then on the options tab select the ascending or descending sort.

March	April	May	June	July	August	September	Oct
37186	55255	55380	46455	134957	158902	130893	21
4824	3973	5666	4927	4233	12557	12083	1
342398	228062	353023	272684	381526	396431	737744	82
384408	287290	414069	324066	520716	567890	880720	105

Figure 406 Sort the Pivot Table

You can apply as much formatting as you wish.

To use some preselected layouts, select any cell in the pivot, and then you will see the Pivot Tables Tools tabs appear. Click on the Design tab and play around until you have the layout you like.

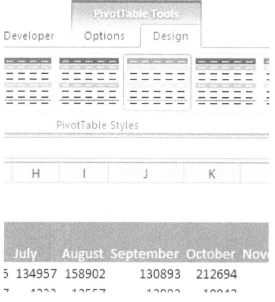

Figure 407 Pivot Table - Contextual Tabs - Design

You can still format individual cells that you select by using the options in the home tab. The general advice is to keep to the preselected design options. They are there because they work well.

There are many other options available in the Design and Layout tabs.

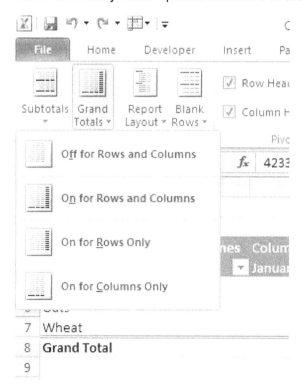

Figure 408 Pivot options - grand totals

All options can be undone, so there is no harm in experimenting to see how your data is best presented.

The power of the pivot is that you can play with your data. This is a simple data set. Perhaps it would look better with the months as rows and the cereals as columns.

	Sum of Quantities sold in tonnes Column Labels ▾			
Row Labels ▾	Barley	Oats	Wheat	Grand Total
January	91913	9674	268064	369651
February	47085	8940	233247	289272
March	37186	4824	342398	384408
April	55255	3973	228062	287290
May	55380	5666	353023	414069
June	46455	4927	272684	324066
July	134957	4233	381526	520716
August	158902	12557	396431	567890
September	130893	12083	737744	880720
October	212694	10942	826523	1050159
November	108273	6950	568829	684052
December	93267	9199	527031	629497
Grand Total	1172260	93968	5135562	6401790

Figure 409 Changing Pivot Table layout

It is simple to just drag and drop the fields in to the respective areas.

Once you have selected a preferred format for your pivot table, you may want to apply it to other data. In the example in Figure 405, use the figures for 2015 on another worksheet.

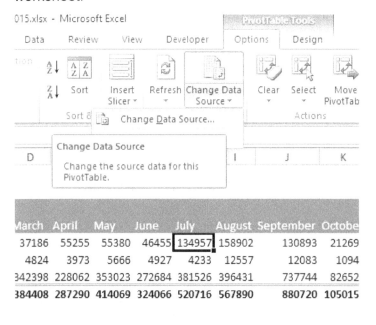

Figure 410 Changing the Pivot Table data source

To change the data source on the options tab, in the data group select change data source.

In Figure 406, the 2014 data is on another worksheet in the same spreadsheet. By selecting that tab, the table range is changed automatically.

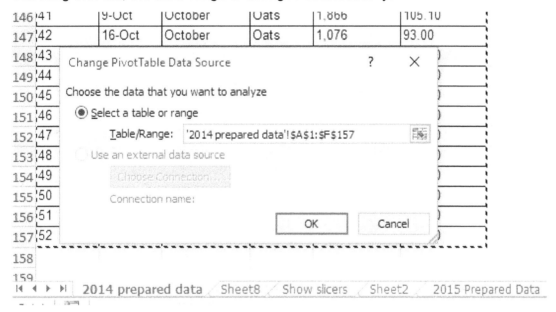

Figure 411 Change the pivot table data source dialogue box

Data can be in another spreadsheet or external source. Click OK to see the new data in your pivot.

Create a Pivot Chart

Instead of showing the data in a table, you can create a Pivot Chart to show the same information but automatically in a graph.

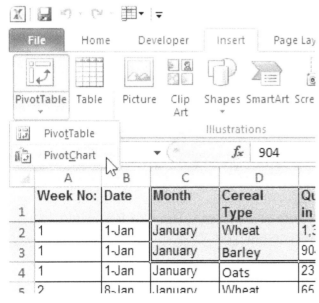

Figure 412 Create a Pivot Chart to display your data

The process is almost the same as creating a Pivot Table. Click a cell in the table of data, then Insert Pivot Chart.

A familiar dialogue box will appear, this time headed Pivot Chart.

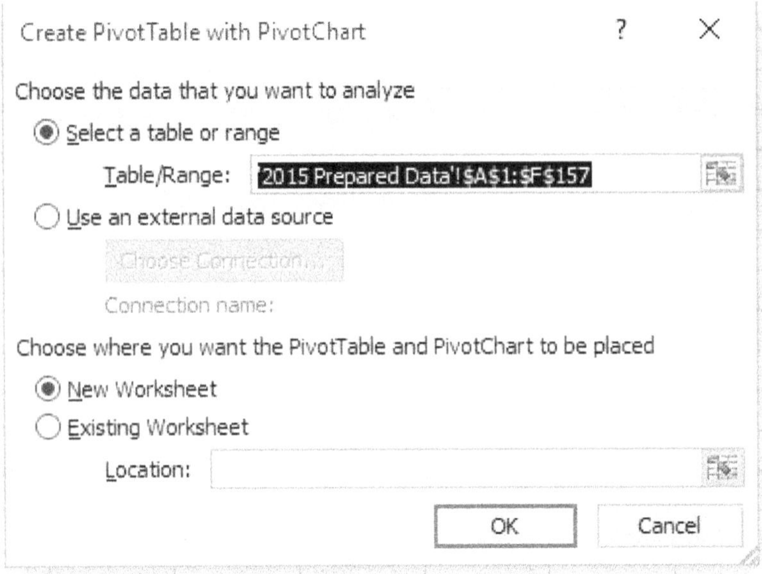

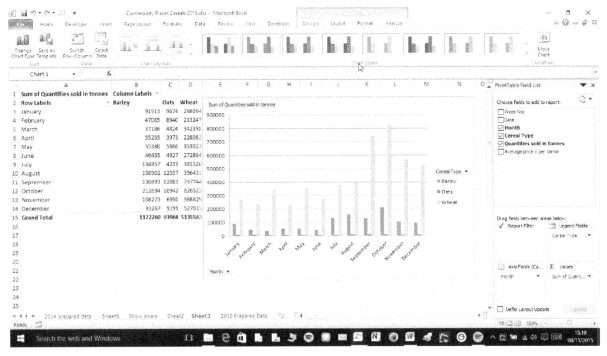

Figure 413 Create a Pivot Table with Pivot Chart

The next screen is also familiar allowing you to develop the pivot.

Figure 414 Pivot Chart field list

In Figure 409 you are comparing, sales of cereals by month. The Axis field is month. The $\sum$ is quantity sold and the legend field is cereal type.

The power of the Pivot is that you can play with the fields, and the layout.

The goal of creating a pivot is to readily allow your audience make sense of the data that you are presenting. In the graph above there is one scale but clearly very different levels of cereal sold. More wheat is sold than barley than oats.

One way to make the trend clearer is to include a SLICER. This is a filter that you add to the pivot.

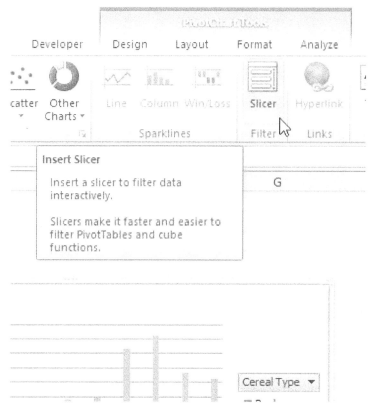

Figure 415 Insert Slicer

On the insert tab, in the Filter group, click slicer. Select the field you wish to filter by. In this case select Cereal Type. Click ok and a new dialogue box appears with the slicers in.

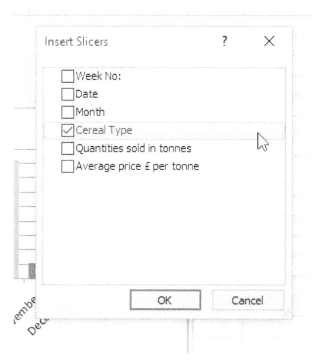

Figure 416 Insert Slicer choose fields

The slicer allows you to click on any one of the filter items.

In figure 412 you can see the annual sales for Barley.

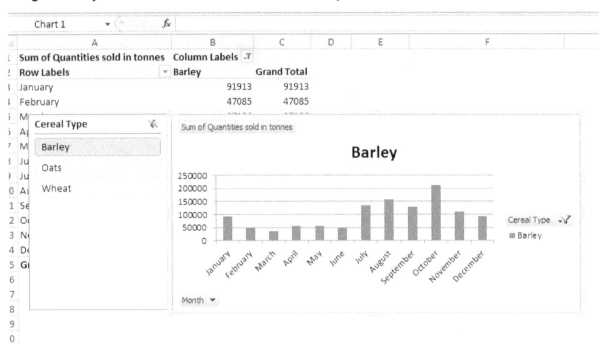

Figure 417 Showing slicer on a pivot chart

Note that the same effect can be achieved by clicking on any of the manual filter icons on the pivot chart.

To restore the original chart, delete the filter by clicking on the filter button.

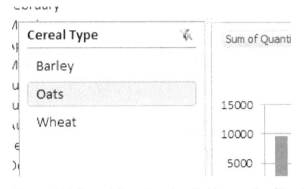

Figure 418 Cancel the slicer by clicking on the filter icon

Slicers equally apply to filtering data. To follow along the following example you may wish to download data from www.england.nhs.uk/statistics/statistical-work-areas/diagnostics-waiting-times-and-activity/imaging-and-radiodiagnostics-annual-data/

In figure 414 shows by area, the number of selected types of medical imaging. With the ability to "drill down" in to the data by individual medical centre.

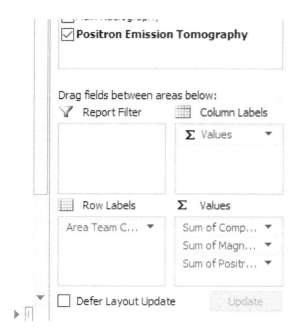

Figure 419 Slicer allowing drilling don in to data

The first step is to create the pivot table. In this case the row labels are Area Codes, the ∑ value are the modalities (type of imaging device) that you wish to look at in detail. The Column Label is automatically populated with the ∑ value (summation value).

The next step is to add the slicer. In figure 415, to filter by area code. This allows you to see the total for each area code.

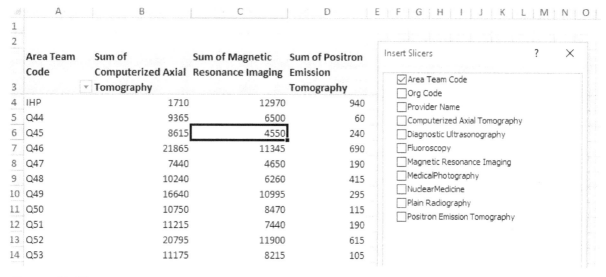

Figure 420 Slicer "by area code"

The next step is to return to the pivot table and to add the second level of filter. In this case we want the Provider Name (the medical centres in each area).

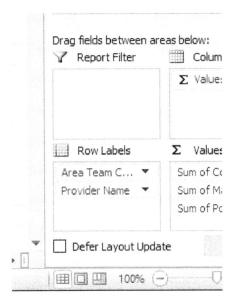

Drag fields between areas below:

Report Filter	Colum...
	Σ Value:

Row Labels	Σ Values
Area Team C... ▼	Sum of Cc
Provider Name ▼	Sum of M;
	Sum of Pc

☐ Defer Layout Update

⊞ ▢ ⊞ 100% ⊖

Figure 421 Insert the second level of filter

As you can see, in any large database that has been sliced in this way, there will be lots of data.

Area Team Code	Sum of Computerized Axial Tomography	Sum of Magnetic Resonance Imaging	Sum of Positron Emission Tomography
⊟ IHP	1710	12970	940
Alliance Medical	0	65	940
BMI Healthcare	255	1560	0
Care UK	0	870	0
Circle	90	265	0
Direct Medical Imaging LTD	0	380	0
InHealth Group Limited	0	5065	0
Molecular Imaging Solutions Limited	0	20	0
Nuffield Health	130	445	0
Peninsula Ultrasound Limited	0	0	0
Prime Diagnostics Limited	0	0	0
Ramsay Healthcare UK Operations Limited	690	2425	0
Spire Healthcare	545	1875	0
Virgin Care Services Ltd	0	0	0
⊟ Q44	9365	6500	60
Countess of Chester Hospital NHS F.T.	1720	1075	0
East Cheshire NHS Trust	1080	685	0
Mid Cheshire Hospitals NHS F.T.	1485	1630	0
The Clatterbridge Cancer NHS F.T.	500	430	0

Area Tea
Q64
Q65
Q66
Q67
Q68
Q69
Q70
Q71

Figure 422 Slicing a large database

You can click on the slicer to select a single area code and to see those medical centres within that area.

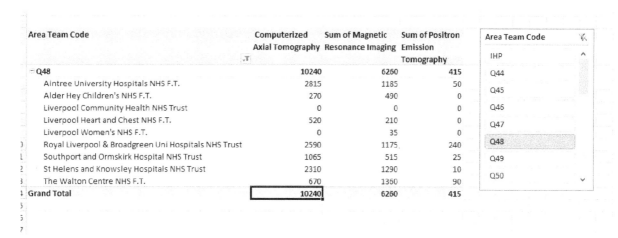

Area Team Code	Computerized Axial Tomography	Sum of Magnetic Resonance Imaging	Sum of Positron Emission Tomography
− Q48	10240	6260	415
Aintree University Hospitals NHS F.T.	2815	1185	50
Alder Hey Children's NHS F.T.	270	490	0
Liverpool Community Health NHS Trust	0	0	0
Liverpool Heart and Chest NHS F.T.	520	210	0
Liverpool Women's NHS F.T.	0	35	0
Royal Liverpool & Broadgreen Uni Hospitals NHS Trust	2590	1175	240
Southport and Ormskirk Hospital NHS Trust	1065	515	25
St Helens and Knowsley Hospitals NHS Trust	2310	1290	10
The Walton Centre NHS F.T.	670	1360	90
Grand Total	10240	6260	415

Figure 423 Sliced to look at just one area

Another way to collapse the volume data is to choose the row label field and then select the Options tab, in the Active Field group click on the collapse entire field.

Figure 424 Collapse Entire Field

This can easily be reversed by clicking the Expand Entire Field.

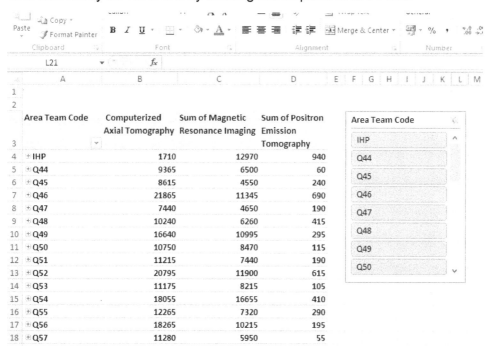

Area Team Code	Computerized Axial Tomography	Sum of Magnetic Resonance Imaging	Sum of Positron Emission Tomography
⊞ IHP	1710	12970	940
⊞ Q44	9365	6500	60
⊞ Q45	8615	4550	240
⊞ Q46	21865	11345	690
⊞ Q47	7440	4650	190
⊞ Q48	10240	6260	415
⊞ Q49	16640	10995	295
⊞ Q50	10750	8470	115
⊞ Q51	11215	7440	190
⊞ Q52	20795	11900	615
⊞ Q53	11175	8215	105
⊞ Q54	18055	16655	410
⊞ Q55	12265	7320	290
⊞ Q56	18265	10215	195
⊞ Q57	11280	5950	55

Figure 425 Expand Entire Field

Chapter 6 Sharing your work

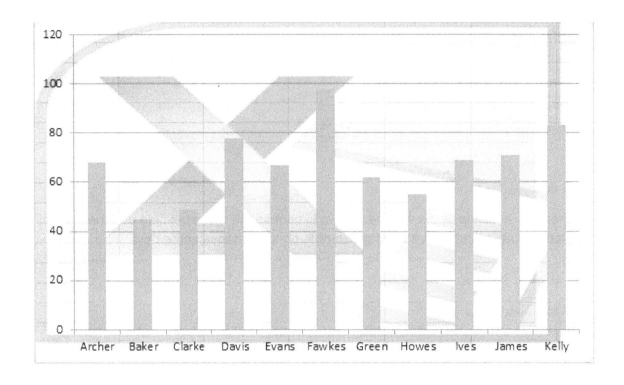

Chapter 6 Sharing your work

There will come a time when you will want to share your spreadsheet with others. This has many benefits and also it can create many issues. This section focuses on these issues and how to resolve them.

It is wise to be very protective of the data that you share. Many people are surprised at what "hidden" information is available in the Office documents that they send. This is known as METADATA. To see this metadata, take a look at the Backstage View. Go to the File tab and click on Info.

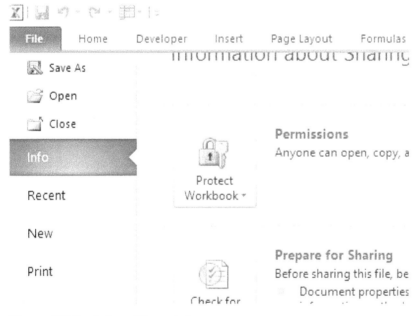

Figure 426 Backstage View – Info

In figure 422, some of the information has been added deliberately to show you what can be recorded. However, much of the information is automatically completed.

Properties ▾

Size	24.8KB
Title	December 2015 information
Comments	(c) Crown Copyright Amended fr...

Comments

(c) Crown Copyright
Amended from publicly available
data. The figures DO NOT
represent real data

Company	Ottershome
IC Description	Add text
Release date	N/A
Order	Add text

Related Dates

Last Modified	Today, 19:27
Created	11/02/2002 15:25
Last Printed	23/07/2004 13:57

Related People

Manager	Charles Eaton
	Specify the manager
Author	Justin Holt
	Add an author
Last Modified By	Justin Holt

Related Documents

Figure 427 Metadata included in a spreadsheet

You might want to look at some of the many files you will have sent and received recently. When someone has told you they have worked all weekend on a document, you can check the information to see exactly how long they were working on it, or if they were the original author.

Before sharing a document you can check it by clicking on the Check For Issues icon in the Info menu on the File Tab. Select Inspect Document.

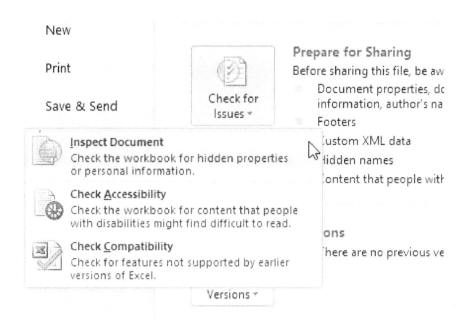

Figure 428 Prepare for Sharing - Inspect Document

There are many options that you can check for. If you are unsure, then check for everything. Click Inspect.

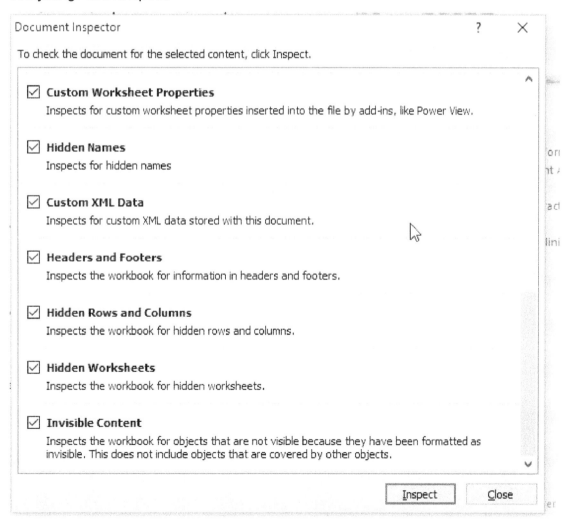

Figure 429 Select content to be checked

The dialogue box will alert you to any potential issues.

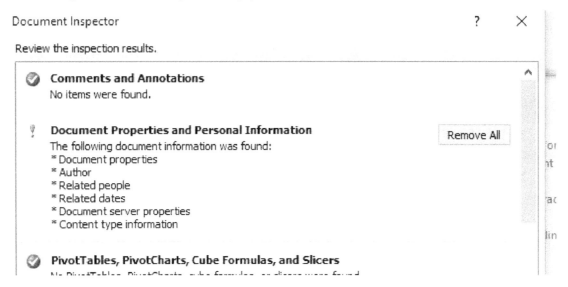

Figure 430 Inspection results

Before you click the Remove All button, note that many changes can't be undone. If you want to keep certain elements of the metadata, either don't click remove all for that section or reinspect the document but deselect that section. When you are certain click Remove All.

Look again at the backstage view and review the changes.

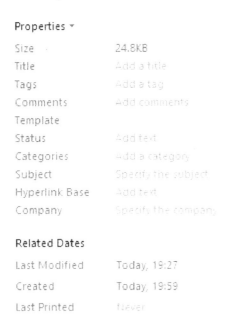

Figure 431 Cleared of selected metadata

When you share a spreadsheet it is almost inevitable someone will break it at some point. One way to save yourself from the grief that will invariably follow is to password protect either the entire work book or just the work sheet.

You may have created complex formulas, defined variables, written macros or even just want to preserve the layout. If you share without restricting access, then these are bound to get changed.

Password protecting your work means that the only people who can alter your document are those who you have given the password to.

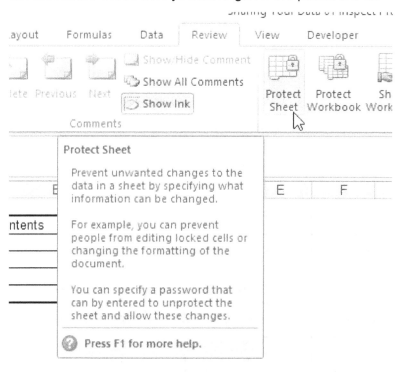

Figure 432 Protect Sheet

To protect your worksheet, go to the Review tab and click on the Protect Sheet button.

Some important password pointers

- They are case sensitive
- Make them secure This means not using the names or date of birth of your kids or the name of your favourite football team
- Try using two or more words with numbers substituted for letters (example H4r0ldH1ll for HaroldHill)
- A moderately determined person can break MS Office password protection. If your data is particularly sensitive and you need extra protection, there are third party suppliers of encryption software

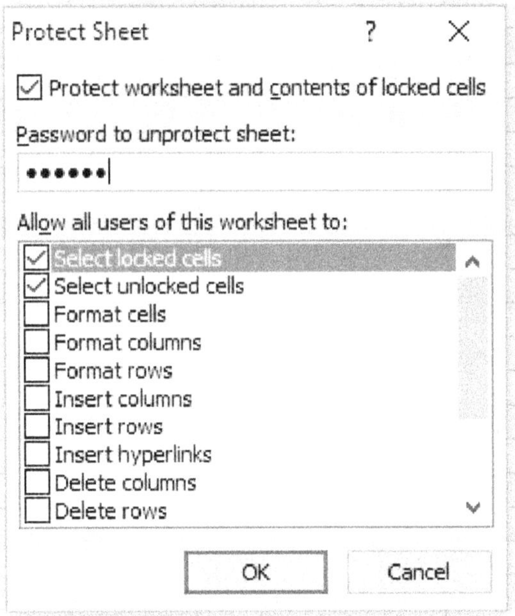

Protect Sheet ? ×

☑ Protect worksheet and contents of locked cells

Password to unprotect sheet:

●●●●●●|

Allow all users of this worksheet to:

☑ Select locked cells

☑ Select unlocked cells

☐ Format cells

☐ Format columns

☐ Format rows

☐ Insert columns

☐ Insert rows

☐ Insert hyperlinks

☐ Delete columns

☐ Delete rows

OK Cancel

Figure 433 Specify what users can do to your shared worksheet

Click OK and you will be asked to confirm your password.

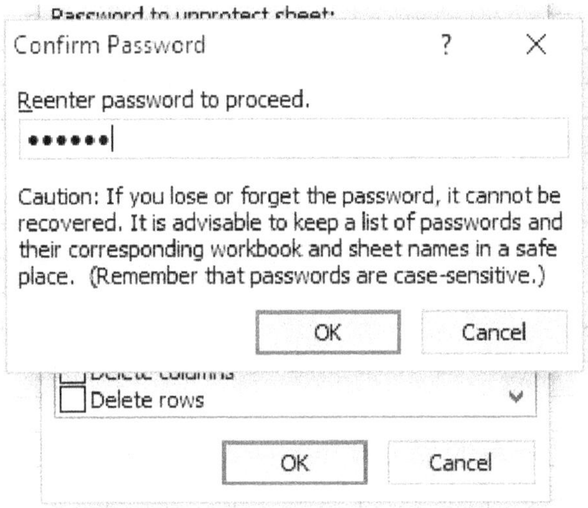

Confirm Password ? ×

Reenter password to proceed.

●●●●●●|

Caution: If you lose or forget the password, it cannot be recovered. It is advisable to keep a list of passwords and their corresponding workbook and sheet names in a safe place. (Remember that passwords are case-sensitive.)

OK Cancel

Delete rows

OK Cancel

Figure 434 Select and confirm a password

It may be worth noting that most security experts don't suggest you do as Microsoft have suggested in this dialogue box. Your list of passwords could be compromised or taken.

When someone attempts to change anything in your document they will get an error message.

Figure 435 Remove protection using a password

They will have to go to the Review Tab and click on unprotect Sheet. They will have to enter the correct password before they can make changes.

Figure 436 Unprotect sheet use password

There will be occasions where you will want to share your spreadsheet and to allow users to change the data in certain cells, while making sure that other cells can't be changed.

A good example of this may be where you want to have a formula in a cell, and don't want that formula to be changed. Protecting cells can seem to be complicated so I will use some simple examples to demonstrate.

In my experience, one reason for this seemingly complicated view is that Microsoft wants you to think about the cells you want to *prevent* data entry in.

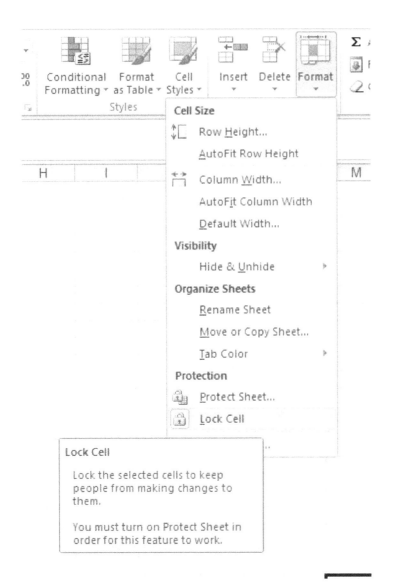

Another way to look at the same problem is to decide which cells you want to *allow* data entry. Try both ways and you can decide which works best for you.

	A	B	C	D	E
1	Region	Sales			
2	North				
3	South				
4	West				
5	East				
6	Total	£0.00			
7					
8		= cells we want unlocked so data can be entered			
9					

In the first demonstration, by following the instructions below, you will prevent then allow access to all cells in a **blank** worksheet.

By default, all cells are protected. This may seem strange, as at this point you can enter data in to any cell you like. However, cell protection only takes effect when the entire sheet is protected. To see this for yourself, create a new blank spreadsheet. You can click in any cell.

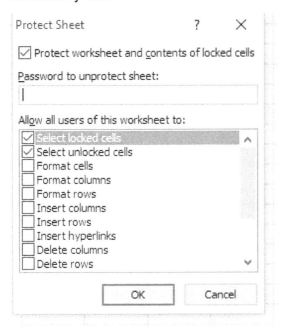

Figure 439 Enter a password to unprotect the sheet in the Protect Sheet dialogue box

Then on the Review tab, click Protect Sheet. You will be presented with the Protect Sheet Dialogue box. Uncheck the Select locked cells box. N.B. If you don't do this, you are allowing "all users of this worksheet to:" select both locked and unlocked cells. This is pretty much the same as not protecting the sheet' Click OK. Now try and select any cell. You can't.
To enable access, unprotect the sheet.
In another blank work sheet, Type the word "Allow" in Cell A1 and in C1. Then type the word "Deny" in A2 and C2. Formatting the cell background may make this demo clearer.

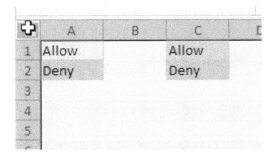

Figure 440 Protect individual cells

Select all the cells. Right click and select format cells.

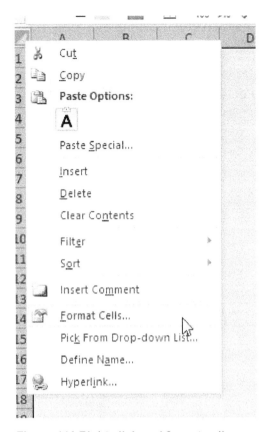

Figure 441 Right click and format cells

Uncheck the Locked check box.

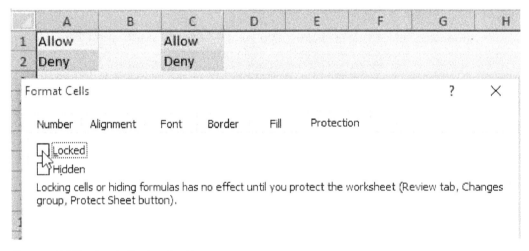

Figure 442 Uncheck the Locked box

This has the effect of making all the cells in the worksheet unlocked.

On the review tab, click on the Protect sheet icon. In the dialogue box, uncheck the Select locked cells checkbox.

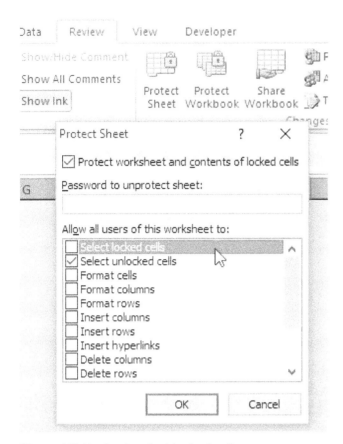

Figure 443 Uncheck select locked cells

Reading the dialogue box we can see that the effect of this will be to NOT "allow all users of the worksheet to … select locked cells". This is correct; we don't want them to select those cells we are specifically protecting. Click OK. At this point you are still able to select any cell.

Unprotect the sheet by clicking the Unprotect Sheet icon. At this point you are still able to select any cell, but the sheet is unprotected.

Select A2 and C2. Right click to bring up the Format Cells.

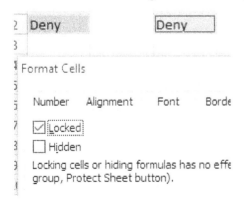

Figure 444 Select two cells and check locked

Check the Locked checkbox. Click OK. At this point you can still select any cell.

In the Review tab, select the Protect Sheet icon and uncheck the Select Locked Cells checkbox. You don't want to allow the locked cells to be able to be edited.

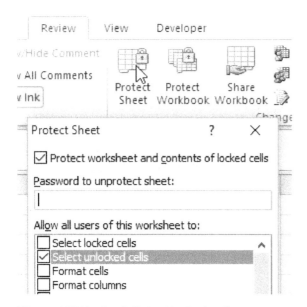

Figure 445 Uncheck Select locked cells

Click OK. At this point you can select ANY cell EXCEPT A2 and C2.

This is an important point. You can select ANY cell except the two cells that have specifically been denied. This means in a real world example, those users who you have shared with can change everything except those few cells. This would be useful to block changes to cells that contain formulas.

The second approach is to consider only those cells that you want to **ALLOW** to be edited. For example, in a large data entry form, you would only want users to enter data in a few selected cells.

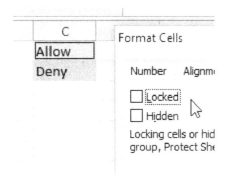

Figure 446 Allowing only selected cells to be editable

The process of protecting the sheet is very similar. Try the steps below to see the difference in action.

As in the previous demo, create a new worksheet with Allow in A1 and C1, and Deny in A2 and C2.

This time please DO NOT select the whole sheet and unlock the cells. This leaves the worksheet in the default state where all cells are set as being locked. (Recall earlier you demonstrated the effect of protecting a sheet of locked cells). DO select cells A1 and C1. Right click bring up the format cells dialogue box.

Uncheck the Locked checkbox.

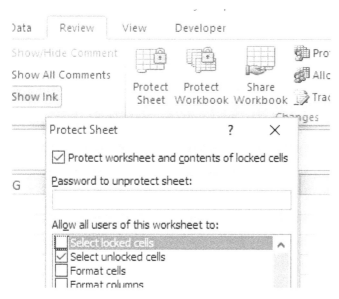

Figure 447 Uncheck locked cells

Click OK. This has the effect of ensuring ONLY specifically unlocked cells are editable.

In this instance, only A1 and C1 can be changed. You can tab between the allowed cells.

The effect of either method is to prevent cells A2 and C2 from being edited.

However, the crucial difference is that in the second demo, ONLY A1 and C1 can be changed.

Play with the differences to see which best suits your spreadsheet. In my experience, there tends to be fewer cells you wish to allow users to change. Generally you won't want them to rename cells.

In Figure 433 showing regional sales figures, with the first method ONLY the formula to sum the four regions is protected. It would be possible to make East North and West South. The second method ensures the only fields that can change are those that you intend to be changed.

Chapter 7 Document your work

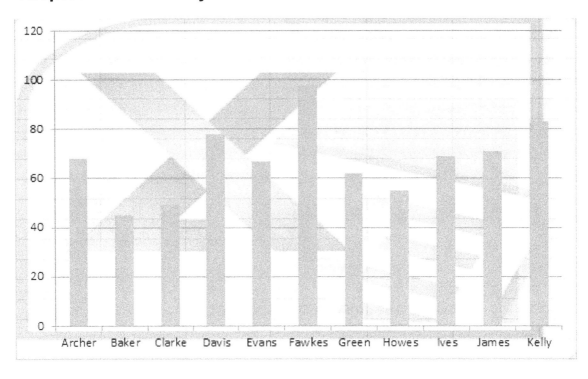

Chapter 7 Document your work

This section is about how to document your spreadsheet.

There are several reasons why this is good practice. You may need to do it for compliance purposes, or because it is the standard required at your workplace. One of the best reasons to document your worksheet is to save time when you have to revisit your work at a later date. What made sense in June may well be incomprehensible in December. Documenting your work may well pay you dividends many times over.

	C	D	E	F	G	H
	Male ▾	Female ▾	Year ▾			
36	2113248	2017388	1992			257,543,525
95	2105722	2010073	1992			260,482,222
32	2095016	1996816	1992			
30	2017188	1924442	1992			
09	1999078	1908731	1992		Yr	$ pa
27	1969823	1877604	1992		1992	22002
19	1959344	1867475	1992		1993	22191

Figure 448 An example of an undocumented worksheet

One of the simplest things you can do is to add a comment on your cells. To enter a comment, click on the cell that you are commenting upon and then use the keyboard shortcut Shift + F2.

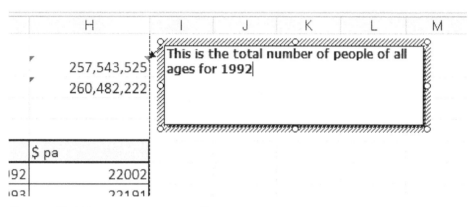

Figure 449 Add a comment to a cell

If you prefer, you can right click in the cell and then INSERT COMMENT. By default, it will have the name of the computer owner already entered. If you don't find that useful, simply overtype. There is no right or wrong way.

The comment box can be stretched or pinched to size and you can change the font as appropriate. The box can be moved to wherever you need it to display.

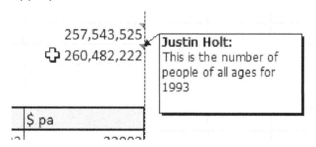

Figure 450 Change the size of the comment box

The comment only appears when you hover your mouse curser over a cell that has a red triangle in the top right hand side.

As you'd expect, you can format the comment by highlighting the text and right clicking.

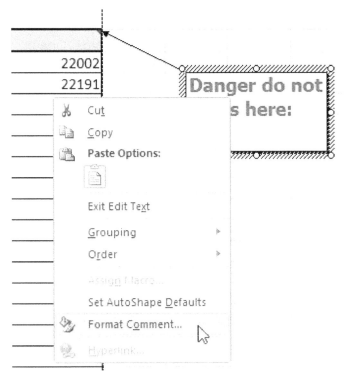

Figure 451 You can format any comment

The comments in this example are simple. However, if you are developing a more complex spreadsheet, you can add comments that would help you understand formulas that make sense now, but could appear unfathomable when you troubleshoot them in a years' time.

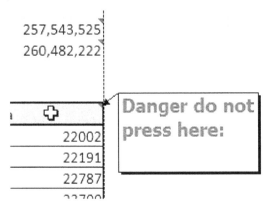

Figure 452 Make your comments as simple or complex as necessary

Another easy way to self-document your spreadsheet is to use named ranges.

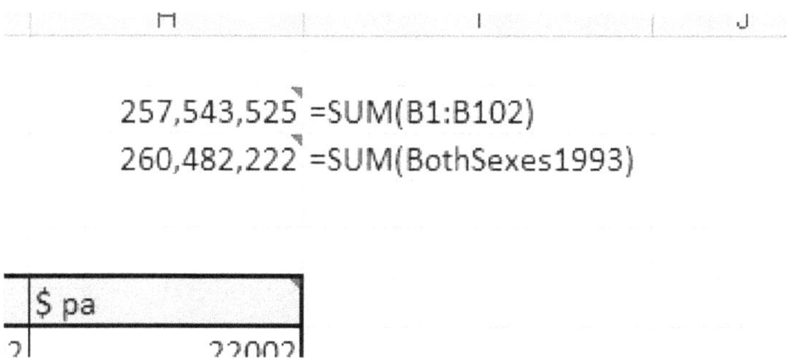

257,543,525 =SUM(B1:B102)

260,482,222 =SUM(BothSexes1993)

$ pa

2   22002

Figure 453 Illustrating named ranges in a formula Vs. cell ranges

Looking at the two formulas, you can easily see which would be easier to troubleshoot. The first result is the total number of people alive in USA in 1992, the second is the total number of people alive in the USA in 1993.

When you share your spreadsheet I recommend that you keep a separate unaltered copy somewhere safe to refer back to in the future.

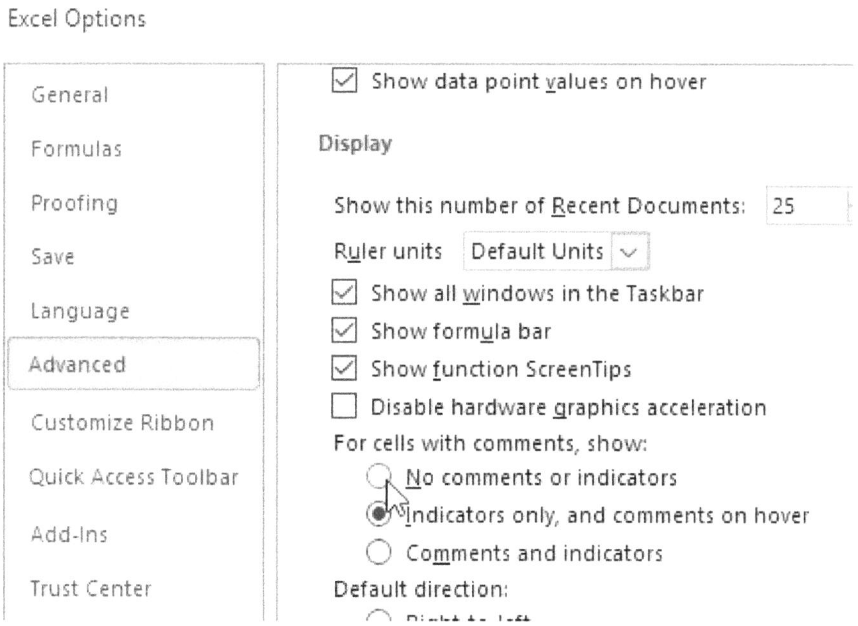

Excel Options

General

Formulas

Proofing

Save

Language

Advanced

Customize Ribbon

Quick Access Toolbar

Add-Ins

Trust Center

☑ Show data point values on hover

Display

Show this number of Recent Documents: 25

Ruler units   Default Units ✔

☑ Show all windows in the Taskbar

☑ Show formula bar

☑ Show function ScreenTips

☐ Disable hardware graphics acceleration

For cells with comments, show:

○ No comments or indicators

◉ Indicators only, and comments on hover

○ Comments and indicators

Default direction:

○ Right to Left

Figure 454 Show Indicators only and comments on hover

In the copy you share, it might not be appropriate to show your comments. They are easy to turn off. In the backstage view, click options then click advanced. Scroll to display. You can select any of three options. The default is to show indicators only and comments on hover. You may prefer your shared spreadsheet to have No Comments or Indicators.

Chapter 8 Create a macro

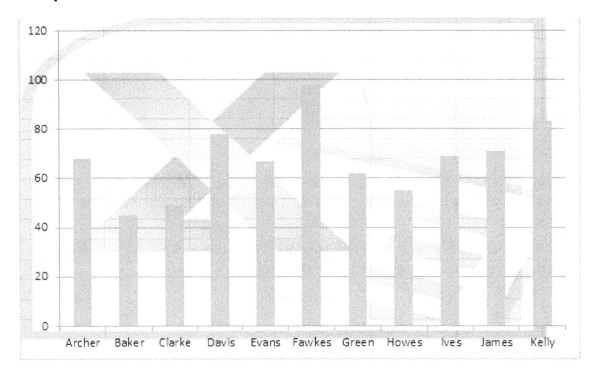

Chapter 8 Create a Macro

The purpose of a macro is to help you automate tasks that you do frequently. It is a set of instructions that Excel will follow every time it is told to execute them. This is known as calling or running your macro.

These instructions are created using Visual Basic for Applications (VBA). How to program using VBA could be an entire book in itself. At this point keep things simple and easy to follow. There is no need to learn how to program.

Excel provides an easy way to create a macro by recording the tasks you want to automate. By following along, you will record a very simple macro and use it. Later you will recreate another more complex set of tasks.

By default, Excel does not display the tools needed. Look at the tabs along the top of a new worksheet. If you don't see one called Developer, then you need to customise your ribbon.

Right click any tab and Customize the Ribbon.

Figure 455 Customise the Ribbon - show the developer tab

Tick the check box for developer. The tab will now appear along with your other tabs.

Figure 456 Check the developer checkbox

In the following example you will create a macro to create a chart of some data. In my example it is for sales by type over a 3 year period.

To follow along with this example, you may want to enter or copy and paste the following in to a new worksheet.

	2014	2015	2016
Motor vehicle and parts dealers	689,679	779,967	816,651
Furniture and home furnishings stores	77,569	85,129	91,352
Electronics and appliance stores	74,686	82,022	87,482
Building material and garden equipment and supplies stores	202,724	264,039	278,109
Food and beverage stores	417,433	442,622	459,185
Health and personal care stores	129,699	145,419	157,468
Gasoline stations	191,887	209,409	244,450
Clothing and clothing accessories stores	149,433	159,888	167,541
Sporting goods, hobby, book, and music stores	68,939	74,045	78,120
General merchandise stores	351,186	381,428	405,936
Miscellaneous store retailers	99,757	105,742	109,000
Nonstore retailers	134,113	138,445	163,844
	2,587,105	2,868,155	3,059,138

This will be the contents of cell A2:D15. Save your file.

Your spreadsheet will currently have a title and extension such as 'MyData.xlsx'. Once you have created your macro and saved the spreadsheet again you will need to save it as a MACRO ENABLED spreadsheet. It will be saved with a different extension and you will see it as 'MyData.xlsm'. Note the change in the extension from xlsx to xlsm.

Figure 457 Record Macro on the Developer tab

To start your macro, click on the Developer tab, then click on Record Macro. Your actions are recorded and translated in to VBA code.

If you make a mistake, you can stop and discard your recording. If it works as you intend you can save the macro and use it again.

You need to give your macro a descriptive name. The default Macro01 isn't very helpful.

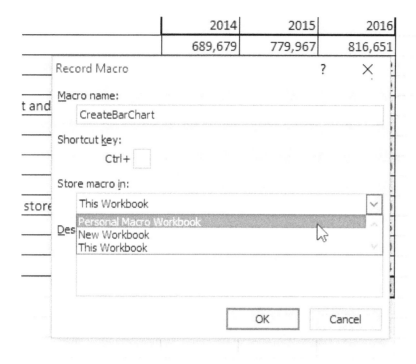

	2014	2015	2016
	689,679	779,967	816,651

Record Macro ? ✕

Macro name:

CreateBarChart

Shortcut key:

Ctrl+

Store macro in:

This Workbook ⌄

Personal Macro Workbook
New Workbook
This Workbook

OK   Cancel

Figure 458 Give your macro a meaningful name

You can assign a shortcut key, so that you can call your macro without using your mouse. As there are already Windows shortcuts, I tend not to use this. For example type Ctrl+P and you are previewing a print. You don't want to overwrite a standard Windows shortcut.

To be used again, the VBA code has to be stored somewhere. The choices are in a Personal Macro Workbook, a New Workbook or This Workbook.

If your macro will be needed by several of your workbooks then you would store it in the Personal Macro Workbook which makes it available everywhere. If the instructions are particular to one spreadsheet then store it in This Workbook.

Do make sure you add a descriptive comment in the box provided. It will help you later.

Click OK.

In this exercise, highlight the data; add a new bar chart and then move it to the right of the data. At this point, click on the developer tab, and select Stop Recording.

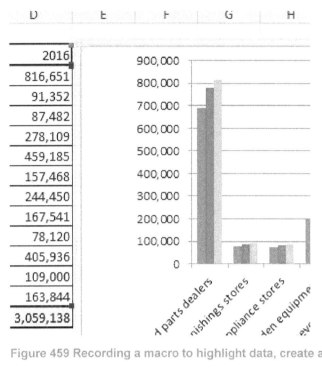

Anytime that you need to create a chart of this data you call your macro.

To look at the code created from your actions click on the developer tab in the code group click on the macro icon. The keyboard short cut is ALT+F8.

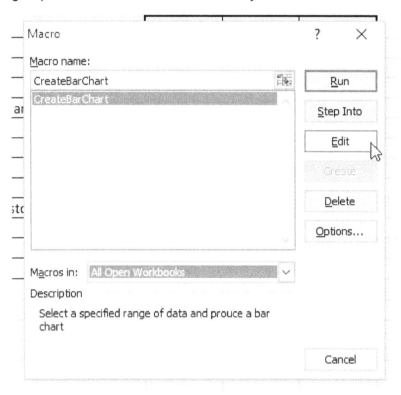

Select the macro and click edit. When you have many macros, giving them descriptive names is so helpful.

This will open the Microsoft Visual Basic window. Don't worry about how complex this appears.

If you know how to code you would be able to customise the macro. You could even write them from scratch. This is out of scope for this text. Just know that your actions while the macro was recording results in a small program that you can call any time you need. Close the window by clicking the X at the top right of the screen.

To run your macro, click on developer tab, click on macro in the code group, then highlight the appropriate macro, and click run. In this example, there is only one, but it could be many more.

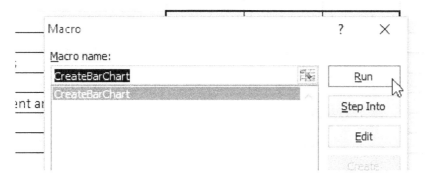

This is a simple example, and there appears to be a lot of work involved just to run a macro.

There has to be an easier way to call your macro? There is. You can add it to the quick access toolbar (QAT).

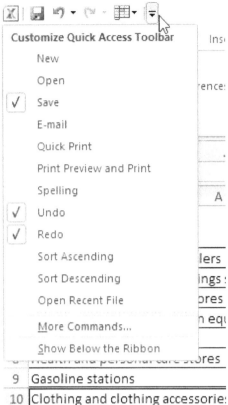

Figure 463 Assign a macro to the Quick Access Toolbar (QAT)

Click on the customise QAT list arrow, and select more commands.

Click on the Choose Commands from list arrow and select Macros.

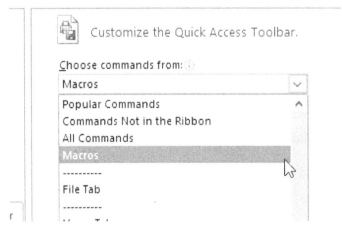

Figure 464 Add to QAT

Click the Add button in the centre and the macro will be added to the QAT.

The macro is now on the QAT. Click the new icon and the chart will be created.

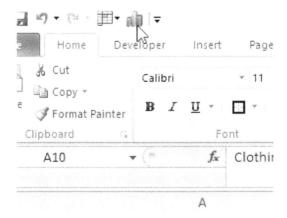

Figure 465 Macro added to QAT

Macros can be as simple or as complicated as you need. For example you could automatically download information published on a website or stored on a company network. This could be stock prices, an equipment price list or exchange rates.

If you wish to follow the example below I am taking data from the UK Barclays Premier League football league table of top goal scorers. The best site is the official (mobile) site http://m.premierleague.com/en-gb/statistics.html

You might want to use the actual league positions. These can be found here

http://www.sfstats.net/soccer/leagues/3_Premiership

The official website can be found here http://www.premierleague.com/en-gb.html but a recent change means that scripts are being run which I find can interfere with importing the data.

Open a new spreadsheet in Excel, and start the macro recorder. Give your macro a meaningful name, save it to your personal workbook and make notes in the description field.

Figure 466 Record a macro to automatically collect data from a website

On the data tab, Get External data, and click the From Web icon.

You will be presented with a dialogue box. In the address field type or copy in the URL of the website where the data is located.

Select the table you wish to take your data from (Tables are indicated by a black arrow on a square yellow background). Click the Import button.

You may find you get messages regarding running scripts. These originate on the website. It is generally safe to not continue running them.

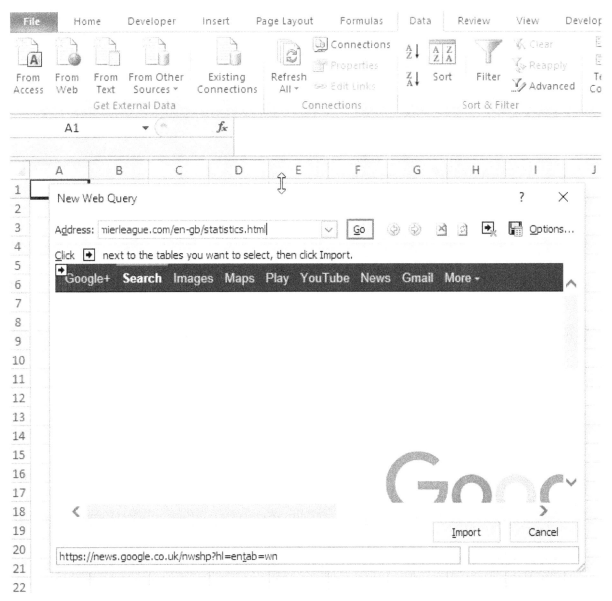

Figure 467 New Web Query

Click Go.

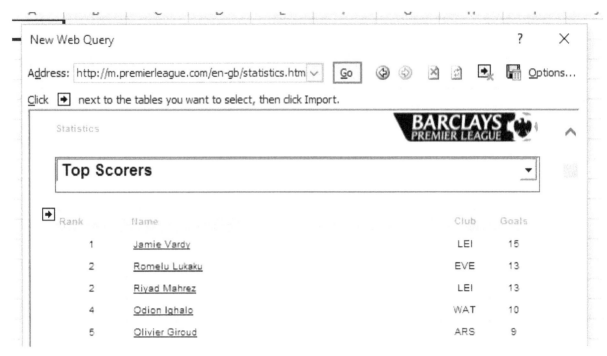

Figure 468 Tables containing importable data are indicated by a black arrow in a yellow square

The next dialogue box requires you to say where you want your data to go.

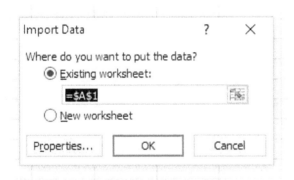

Figure 469 Import data to a specific location on your worksheet

	A	B	C	D
1	Rank	Name	Club	Goals
2	1	Jamie Vardy	LEI	15
3	2	Romelu Lukaku	EVE	13
4	2	Riyad Mahrez	LEI	13
5	4	Odion Ighalo	WAT	10
6	5	Olivier Giroud	ARS	9
7	5	Harry Kane	TOT	9
8	7	Sergio Agüero	MCI	7
9	7	Georginio Wijnaldum	NEW	7
10	9	André Ayew	SWA	6

Figure 470 Data imported to workbook

Stop recording the macro (click on the developer tab, and select Stop Recording). You can of course add this to the Quick Access Toolbar.

You have seen two very simple examples of macros. They can be far more complex.

I was recently told by a local business man, that I had saved him roughly a day a month by automating the processing of his downloaded bank transactions in the form of a CSV file in to a formatted cash sheet.

The key is to create a macro when you find yourself regularly repeating the same tasks. If they are very simple, you may not want to create and run a macro. There is no hard and fast rule.

Chapter 9 Index

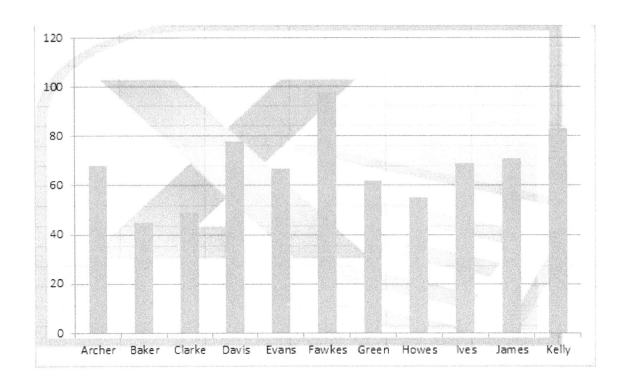

www.ingramcontent.com/pod-product-compliance
Lightning Source LLC
Chambersburg PA
CBHW081225050326
40689CB00016B/3688